A CRACK IN THE TEACUP

C P HOFF

ILLUSTRATED BY
MICHELLE FROESE

PRAISE FOR A CRACK IN THE TEACUP

A pitch-perfect blend of childlike innocence and Mark Twain–style fabulist humour. Hoff very intentionally crafts the events of her narrative in the soft glow of nostalgia, not only for the sweet simplicity of childhood, but also for the comparative innocence of small-town life half a century ago. She writes Celia in a deft register right between those two sentiments: sharp as an adult but with the hilarious viewpoints and priorities of a child.

A fast-paced, funny, and ultimately enchanting story of a little girl's adventures in small-town America.

—*Kirkus Reviews* (starred review)

THE HAPPY VALLEY CHRONICLES
BOOK TWO

All the characters in this book are fictitious, and any resemblance to actual persons, living or dead, is purely coincidental.

Editor - Adrienne Kerr

Copy editor - Elizabeth McLachlan

Cover design - Stuart Bache

Illustrator - Michelle Froese

Copyright © 2022 by C P Hoff

All rights reserved.

No part of this book may be reproduced in any form or by any electronic or mechanical means, including information storage and retrieval systems, without written permission from the author, except for the use of brief quotations in a book review.

For Kate
My own little Celia

For Chaddy. Thanks for all the sketchbooks, crayons, and inspiration growing up. M.F.

If you like this book, tell a friend; if not, forget you read it.
　Black Crow Books

BOOKS BY CP HOFF

The Picaresque Narratives

West of Ireland

A Town Called Forget

The Happy Valley Chronicles

Canterberry Tales

A Crack in the Tea-Cup

Midnight Hags

Between the Crosses

Happy Valley Picture and Colouring Books

So You Think You're A Pirate

Colouring with Griggs I

1

"I don't think Captain Ahab would approve," I said, leaning on the ironing board. "Sailors never starch, it's against the rules. Besides Queegueg chafes."

Nan rolled her eyes. She'd stopped caring about Captain Ahab's opinion the day my best friend Archibald and me played on my sailboat bed and tried to harpoon her with sharpened willow sticks. Nan was furious. I'd never seen her that mad for such a petty thing. But when it came right down to it, it was her fault. She was the one who insisted on reading me the classics. She could have read me *Hop on Pop* or *Danny and the Dinosaur*, like the sensible parents of the kids in my class, but she said she'd rather gouge out her eyes with a spoon.

I remember the first time I traced a finger over the embossed letters on her copy of *Moby Dick*. They rose and fell under my touch like little waves. When Nan cleared her throat and read the words 'Call me Ishmael,' I almost gasped. Who wouldn't want to be called Ishmael? But that wasn't the only discovery I made. A whole raft of hard-nosed brutes swaggered between those pages.

Nan's regular book-reading voice was almost as good as

Old Lady Griggs' comic-strip-reading one. Except Nan didn't have a plastic-covered chesterfield, so I could listen without worrying about my skin peeling off when I stood up. Griggs and I became thick as thieves last summer when Nan took a job at the druggist's and had her look after me. That's how I learned that Oswald Elliot, Happy Valley's newspaperman, had created a comic strip starring yours truly, detailing my exploits after my should-have-been parents abandoned me at the hospital maternity ward. My very existence was a scandal in town, and Griggs was the one who showed me just how infamous I was.

When Nan got to Queequeg, shivers ran down my spine. I knew I'd never have a braver storybook friend, that he'd accompany me anywhere I wanted to go and never breathe a word of it. Despite all his attributes, though, Nan's lips tightened whenever I brought him up. The harpooning incident had soured her on him for good.

The more I talked of Queequeg chafing, the more Nan starched. She should have known that trying to make me look perfect on the first day of second grade wouldn't make any difference. All the moms dropping off kids would still sniff and turn their backs on me, and the kids—those that didn't have spitballs at the ready—would thumb their noses and run to tell a teacher things I hadn't even thought about doing yet. Besides, who was Nan to judge my appearance, standing in the middle of the kitchen in her housecoat and curlers? She wasn't even wearing any support garments.

"Celia," she said, brandishing the iron, "try to keep clean for at least five minutes."

I spritzed the iron to make it hiss. "Which five? The first or the last? Cause if it's the first, that's easy. Even Queequeg could do that. He could do it with his eyes closed. But if it's the last five minutes, you might as well ask for the moon."

Nan's nostrils pinched together as she handed me my crisp white shirt. "Sometimes, child, you try my patience."

I spritzed once more for good measure. "Sometimes?" I sighed, knowing Nan wasn't being entirely truthful.

Nan turned and headed upstairs, and I padded after her. With all the starching, we were a little behind schedule, and if we didn't hurry, we'd miss the first bell. I wanted to tell Nan she should be more organized, but she'd only blame me. Say that if I hadn't used my new cotton shirt as an earthworm way station she wouldn't have spent half the night bleaching and scrubbing out the marks.

I huffed out all the exasperation that was building in me as I pulled back the sail on my sailboat bed. A brand new pink plaid suspender skirt was waiting for me on the bedspread. I ran a finger over the criss-crosses. Nan had ordered it from the Simpsons-Sears catalog. It didn't look as special on my bed as it had on the girl with the staple through her cheek, all twirly and innocent. Nan and her wishful thinking.

Next to the skirt was a pair of white knee socks. Coupled with the starched shirt I was holding, it was a cute and unassuming ensemble. I hoped it might lull my new teacher into letting down her guard. It was an admirable plan, if not a lofty one.

All summer long, worry about my new teacher had been bubbling in the back of my mind, when I wasn't saving earthworms or burying one of Archibald's dads. (Archibald's mom had a string of unlucky husbands. Old Lady Griggs said they were lightning rods when it came to attracting peculiar deaths, like they were in a competition to get in the book of Guinness World Records. Oswald Elliot wrote a comic strip about Archibald and her assorted fathers too. I was a bit jealous when I found out, but I got over it.)

What if my new teacher was like my old one, Miss Dobbs,

who was boy-crazy for Oswald Elliot (yuck) and smelled like pee? (Double-yuck.) What if she sat in the staffroom with the other teachers, chain-smoking cigarettes and laying bets on which child would be the first to hear the words *turn to your left* in a police lineup? For teachers, that was as fun as shooting craps. And worse than that, what if my new teacher made me sit in the front row where she could whack me with her yardstick?

When I'd fastened my last suspender button, I ventured into Nan's room. She was examining herself in her bureau mirror. She was wearing the same outfit she'd worn on my first day of grade one: the forest green and florescent pink Fortrel sheath dress. I flopped down on her bed, as casual as can be. "We'll walk slow," I said, picking at her tufted chenille bedspread. "Wouldn't want anything to bust loose."

Nan stood on her toes to examine herself more thoroughly. Her brow furrowed, and I knew what she was thinking. After the debacle with my should-have-been parents last summer—the derelicts who tried to blackmail Nan into giving up her house—Nan took to calisthenics and brisk walks. She said the younger she stayed, the easier it would be to keep disaster at bay. Even Old Lady Griggs noticed that Nan had firmed up a fair amount. Said Nan would waste away if she dropped another twenty-five pounds. She was right; Nan looked better in that sheath dress than she had last year, but I couldn't let her know that. I had my reasons.

Nan's laundry business had dwindled to almost nil because of those newfangled automatic washers and tumble dryers everyone was buying, hence her part-time job at the druggist's this summer. Spritzing while she ironed was one of my favourite pastimes, but because I didn't get to do it so much anymore, I took to spritzing Nan when she did her jumping jacks. In one of my spritzing frenzies it occurred to me that if

Nan wanted to be more youthful, the age spots had to go. And if bleach worked on my Nan's whitest whites, why not on Nan? I practiced flicking bleach on the back of her forest green and pink Fortrel sheath dress. Where the stuff hadn't burned right through, whiteish, colourless blotches appeared. But to tell Nan that now was inadvisable.

Nan twisted once more in the mirror but couldn't see her full backside. I had no choice; I had to push the point. "Old Lady Griggs said that sometimes old people bloat for no apparent reason."

"I'm not old." Nan gave her skirt a tug, but I knew she was having second thoughts.

"Have it your way." I shrugged and rolled onto my back. "But don't blame me if there's another Miss Dobbs incident."

By the way Nan's eyes flashed, I saw the seed was sown. Nan made her way to the closet and started shifting the hangers. No one wanted to be like Miss Dobbs, my unfortunate first grade teacher. On the first day of school last year, she slipped in what Timmy Crybaby-Head's mom called "a hallway incident." Everybody else's mom said it was Crybaby-Head's pee. As Miss Dobbs slid along the linoleum floor, her form-fitting pencil skirt split at the seam, exposing her Playtex Living girdle. Nan said the only good thing about the debacle was that it brought her down a couple of pegs.

When Nan finished her primping, we were off. We'd almost made it through the schoolyard when I was overcome. The Happy Valley School for Reluctant Children was right next to the Happy Valley Penitentiary, a bleak monolith of grey stone. Mayor Forde said its proximity was an object lesson for delinquents with sloppy grades, and a cost-saving measure since the side-by-side institutions shared a chain-link fence topped with razor wire.

They added the razor wire to the penitentiary side when

Dinky Farmickel hopped the divider to play hopscotch with his niece, Pew Pew Petunia. That got the entire town debating the safety of the schoolchildren, and some even threatened to vote Mayor Forde out of office. Eventually, they decided against it, because Mayor Forde was the *God-appointed* mayor. And since Dinky didn't mean any harm and hadn't flashed any of the children, most folks concluded it was the most thoughtful thing a man could do—play with a shunned child, that is, not break out of the clink. Dinky, who hadn't finished the sixth grade, fit right in, hopscotching in his prison stripes like there was no tomorrow.

Even with the extra razor wire, my knees buckled. I'd promised myself that I wasn't going to look, that I wasn't going to make a thorough search of the prison yard, but with all the men over in the Happy Valley Penitentiary clamouring to wish students luck on the first day of the new school year, I had to see if my should-have-been pa was in the mix. I scanned the fenceline with my beady eyes for a scraggily man with butter-covered teeth. He was nowhere in sight. Relief and disappointment filled me in equal measure; relief that he wasn't nearby, and disappointment that he was free as a bird after trying to cheat Nan out of her house.

Nan squeezed my hand, so I knew she was as anxious as I was. We quickened our pace to the door of the Happy Valley School for Reluctant Children. I perused the hall. Archibald had to be somewhere in the free-for-all, it was just a matter of ferreting her out. With Nan so close at hand, yelling was out of the question; she didn't care for raised voices indoors. Without knowing where Timmy Crybaby-Head was piddling, jumping was not advised either. One slip, and all Nan's ironing and starching would be out the window.

That's when I heard a familiar yowl and I knew Archibald was adjusting her bolty neck and getting ready to Frankenstein-walk towards me—our preferred greeting since first grade. I adjusted my own imaginary neck bolt and began dragging my leg behind me. It was only a matter of bouncing off bigger kids until we found each other. It didn't take long. Archibald came drooling and lurching from around Mrs. Hoopenmire, Leonard's mom.

"I'm so glad to see you, Celia," Archibald cried. "It's been a terrible summer for earth worms." She held me in a long embrace.

I nodded. "Yes. It's caused me and Nan no end of worry. Nan says the weather's not fit for man or beast. Old Lady Griggs said if we were smart we'd build an ark."

"I'm with Mrs. Griggs. You know, Queequeg is an excellent sailor."

I wanted to tell Archibald that Queequeg couldn't sail an ark, that arks were for plodding along and blundering into mountains, and Queequeg only had experience maneuvering whaling ships on the high seas, but how could Archibald know? She didn't have a sailboat bed; she'd never fixed her sheets to her curtain rod or braved the waves alongside Captain Ahab. She'd never polished peg legs at midnight either. Worst of all, she didn't have a Nan who read her the classics. Her mother was too busy with Archibald's long line of brothers, and those never-ending funeral arrangements. Considering these things, I let it slide. I had bigger fish to fry.

Looking around the crowded hallway, I spied Miss Dobbs pinching cheeks and patting heads. "I wonder if she still smells like pee," I said, raising an eyebrow.

"Let's go have a sniff." There was more excitement in Archibald's voice than I'd heard in some time. Considering the summer she'd had, I would do anything to make her happy.

Adjusting our bolty necks, we waved goodbye to Nan, and drooled our way towards our first grade teacher.

Miss Dobbs glared at both Archibald and me, which was odd. Usually, she saved her hairy eyeball for me alone.

"You're back," she said, with no love in her voice.

I stepped aside, wondering if her tone would change if only Archibald occupied her sight line.

Miss Dobbs scowled even more.

"That's no way to greet students," I said, stepping back towards Archibald.

"Isn't it?"

I shook my head. "No. I've been watching. You've been patting heads and pinching cheeks. Aren't we going to get the same treatment?"

A sly smile crossed Miss Dobbs' face as she leaned over and took hold of Archibald's cheek. Archibald winced. "Happy?" Miss Dobbs asked.

I said nothing. Something had happened since first grade to change Miss Dobbs' feelings about Archibald. A year ago, she would have placed Archibald on a feather pillow if she'd had one. Archibald was like Sarah Crewe from *The Little Princess*, and Miss Dobbs the doting Becky. I looked from Miss Dobbs to Archibald. Archibald blinked up at Miss Dobbs as if she was melting inside. I was missing something.

"You're both in the second grade now. You can't expect to be treated like babies any longer."

"We're in Mrs. Carson's class," Archibald said, reaching for my hand.

Miss Dobbs' lips twitched. "Yes, well, there's been a change of plans. Mrs. Carson has spent the better part of the summer at Souris Valley. Doc Marley sent her there after an office misunderstanding. Once she gets out, she'll be in charge of the grade threes. Less medication needed for that bunch, who are more docile than you ragamuffins."

"Oh," I said, a little excited at being called a ragamuffin.

"Are we going to be left to our own devices? When Nan takes a bath, she sometimes leaves me to my own devices."

Miss Dobbs went white and looked like she would cry. "I should be so lucky. Principal Wolfe isn't of the same mind. He said since I'm familiar with all the students, and to ease the transition, he's moved me up to the second grade. And those lovely grade ones, the innocents I've looked forward to all summer, get some upstart that has never even swung a yardstick."

Archibald almost fell over, so I put my arm around her waist to steady her. "That's wonderful," I said, not meaning it.

No matter how I considered my new predicament, there was no upside. The idea of another year with Miss Dobbs made my throat go dry and my lips stick together. I thought back to Griggs and me last summer. The two of us sitting on her plastic covered chesterfield going over how dismal grade one had been. "I'm not sure where it went wrong," I said. "Nan wore her good occasion lipstick on my first day, and told Miss Dobbs that I was an excellent reader and that she wouldn't have any problems in that department. But Miss Dobbs hated me right away.

"She was slipping the last safety pin in the rip of her pencil-peed skirt," I told Griggs, "when she told Nan that she was sure I was amazing, but she'd take over my education from now on. That Nan needn't be troubling herself. All smiles, Miss Dobbs clip-clopped Nan to the door. When the door shut, she rolled her eyes and said, loud enough for all the class to hear, "What does a doddering old spinster know about teaching a child to read?"

I had put my head on Griggs' shoulder at the memory. "I thought all first grade teachers loved their students. Particularly the girls. That they made dandelion chains at recess and played hopscotch before pricking their fingers to become blood sisters."

Griggs sighed. "In a perfect world, that *would* be the case, but this is Happy Valley." She bent over and hauled out the big black scrapbook she kept under her chesterfield. "And disappointment is baked into your back story. There's a good reason Miss Dobbs' doesn't care for you—your mother, Audrey." She flipped through the pages. "Ah. Here it is. The Origins of the Canterberry family. I'm no fan of Oswald Elliot, but he does his research." After a few throat exercises, Griggs began to read an old comic strip I'd never seen before.

Caroline Dobbs is an ordinary child. She walks ordinary, talks ordinary and sits in her ordinary desk, as any good student should. A teacher's pet in the making. But rosy days aren't on the horizon for poor Caroline Dobbs. Enter stage left, Audrey Canterberry, a wild-eyed girl who's anything but ordinary. She spits, she chews tobacco, and her language—well, this prestigious newsman won't lower himself to print it.

The first time Audrey claps eyes on Caroline, her lip curls up into the most unnatural snarl. "Caroline, teeter-totter with me."

Caroline's eyes widen in horror. "No, thank you."

"I wasn't asking." Grabbing hold of the uncooperative girl, Audrey drags her across the playground to the base of the dreaded apparatus. "Sit," she barks.

Caroline hesitates. To her, a teeter-totter represents splinters and dizzying heights. She can't bear the thought.

Taking a swift jab to the solar plexus, Caroline crumples onto the end of the board and before she has time to recover, is suspended in mid-air by the obstreperous Audrey. "Farmer Brown, Farmer Brown let me down!" Caroline shrieks the international teeter-totter code of submission, but hard-hearted Audrey Canterberry doesn't yield, thumbing her nose at convention. As cool as a cucumber, Audrey examines her nails. "What will you give me if I let you down?"

On the verge of hysterics, Caroline pulls at her once-pristine ponytail. "My lunch? You can have my lunch."

"Got my own."

"My barrettes?" *Her hands tremble as she unclips them from her hair.*

"Wouldn't be caught dead in butterfly barrettes. Now if they were skull and crossbones, we might have a deal."

"My favourite socks?" *She lifts a leg that is not yet shapely.*

"I'll pass."

Whatever she offers, it is not enough. Sadly, for Caroline Dobbs, it is only the first day of her misery. Countless others follow. When a new boy starts school, Audrey wraps him around her little finger before Caroline can get her shoes on. When Caroline wears something special, Audrey spoils it. How long will their rivalry continue? Only time, and the Happy Valley Journal, will tell.

"So you see," Griggs said, closing the scrapbook, "your first day of school wasn't the first time Miss Dobbs laid eyes on you. Not the real you anyway. Oh, she's likely seen you around town, wandering aimlessly, but I doubt that's what's fueled her wrath. Like it or not, you look a bit like your should-have-been ma Audrey, especially around the eyes. How could Caroline Dobbs forget the face of her grade school nemesis?" Griggs leaned back on her plastic covered chesterfield and sighed. "I think Caroline took one look at you and all her school memories came flooding back. And believe you me, none of them were good."

"What did Nan do about Audrey's bullying?"

"Not enough. She was furious, of course. Horrified her daughter would behave in such a way. But try as she might, she couldn't stop her. She warned Audrey, then grounded her, but no matter what she tried, Audrey didn't care. That's why as soon as your Nan found out Caroline was going to be your grade one teacher, she made sure you could read and write. I think she hoped lightening her load would make up for your should-have-been's sins."

But it hadn't. And now Archibald and me were paying the price. Puffing out my cheeks, I looked at Archibald before we both trudged after Miss Dobbs into the classroom with our hearts in our shoes. I didn't know if we'd ever hold hands and swing our arms again.

"At least Miss Dobbs doesn't smell like pee this year," I whispered.

"Not yet," Archibald replied grimly.

2

Archibald slumped in her seat as I took the one behind her. It wasn't a pleasant view. In first grade, one of Archibald's many awards had been for best posture. Some days I thought Miss Dobbs made up awards on the spot, just so she and Archibald could have a special moment. Now it seemed hard to believe. Archibald put her head on her desk, sobbing before the first school bell. No one sobbed before the first bell. It usually took a couple of classes before Miss Dobbs brought someone to tears.

I leaned forward and patted her on the back. "What happened?" I asked, narrowing my eyes at Miss Dobbs. Now I was Jane Eyre and Archibald was Helen Burns. "Miss Scatcherd didn't make you stand on a stool and call you a liar, did she?"

She sniffed. "Who's Miss Scatcherd?"

Sometimes Archibald's lack of literary prowess infuriated me. "Never mind."

Archibald turned in her seat. "It's over," she wailed between snot bubbles. "I'm not Miss Dobbs' favourite anymore." She said it as if it were the worst thing that could happen.

"Why would you want to be?"

"I don't know. Last year I was her pet without hardly trying. Now she won't even look at me."

It was hard for me to sympathize. Miss Dobbs was my number two unspoken nemesis. Mrs. Whitford, the druggist's wife, who looked down on my Nan as one of her husband's employees, was my number one. As for Miss Dobbs, it was only natural that she hate my best friend as well. In fact, I was relieved that she'd started to. It would stop Archibald from waxing on about her, a topic that made my eyes glaze over. All I could do was look at Archibald and shrug. "Easy come, easy go."

"She's mad because my mom won't date her brother. He came by last night with an armful of roses. When my mom opened the door she said, '*Oh god, not you*,' and he looked like he would cry. Miss Dobbs was waiting in the car, smoking with the windows rolled down. She heard everything."

"That doesn't sound so bad," I said. "At least she called him God."

Archibald sniffled. She turned back in her seat and sat as straight as she could, probably to remind Miss Dobbs of the good old days. That's when there was a knock at the classroom door. Miss Dobbs clip-clopped across the room, all eyes on her.

"Yes?" she said, opening the door a crack. The hallway voice was muffled. "Well, aren't you as pretty as a picture," Miss Dobbs said, her voice changing from clipped to syrupy sweet. She opened the door all the way and a cute little pixie girl waltzed in, followed by Mrs. Whitford.

I stiffened. The girl was wearing the same outfit I was, the one Nan bought me from the Simpsons-Sears catalog, except on her it looked adorable. It must have had something to do with her ribbon-tied pigtails and perfectly placed freckles. The kind of granddaughter Nan would have had if she were lucky. I wanted to spit. I knew both of Mrs. Whitford's idiot daughters, and this new girl wasn't either of them. I narrowed my eyes and examined her more thoroughly.

"Class." Miss Dobbs stood next to Mrs. Whitford at the front of the room, her hands on the shoulders of the pixie girl in front of her. "We have a new student. Eugenia Whitford. I want you all to make her feel welcome."

Eugenia flashed an adorable smile, and I thought Miss Dobbs would dissolve on the spot. There was no doubt about it, she had a new class pet. Archibald's shoulders quaked.

Eugenia took her seat at the front of the row, the seat Miss Dobbs made Archibald vacate. "She's warmed it up for you," Miss Dobbs said, as we all moved one seat back.

Eugenia blinked and tilted her head.

"Oh, don't be bashful. No one minds."

Archibald was trembling with all her not minding, but Miss Dobbs didn't seem to notice. She only had eyes for Eugenia.

"First things first. Let's start with introductions." Miss Dobbs wrote her name on the chalkboard. "And then everyone can take turns talking about what they did during the summer. Eugenia, you can start."

Eugenia stood and smoothed her skirt. "My name is Eugenia Whitford. We sold our house in Saskatoon, packed all our things into cardboard boxes and moved here, to be near my aunt and uncle." She gazed adoringly at Mrs. Whitford.

"That sounds terribly exciting," Miss Dobbs purred.

"It was!" Eugenia made it sound like she'd been on some midnight adventure. I hated her already.

Mrs. Whitford, as if on cue, slipped out of the classroom, waving and blowing at least a dozen kisses in Eugenia's direction.

"Next," Miss Dobbs resumed.

I bit my lip and looked at Archibald. It was her turn. And even though I could only see the back of her head, I knew she was blinking back tears. "As I was saying to Archibald earlier," I said without raising my hand, "it's been a particularly poor year for earthworms."

Miss Dobbs rolled her eyes and looked at the clock. "Celia, we've been in class for less than ten minutes and you've already started acting up. I can't spend another year discussing proper weather conditions for the North American earthworm population. It might give Eugenia the wrong impression. We don't want her to go home and tell her recently widowed father that her devoted teacher had no classroom control." She cupped Eugenia's chin in her palm. "That just wouldn't do, now would it?"

I let out a deep breath. "I don't want to discuss it all year, just this morning. Archibald and I spent the summer rescuing as many as we could. We even had an earthworm registry, focusing on distinguishing marks and family groupings."

Archibald nodded emphatically as Miss Dobbs stepped away from Eugenia and slapped a ruler on my desk. "New rule. No talk of earthworms or garden slugs or gluttonous robins. Do I make myself clear?"

"But I was just trying to help Archibald. Besides earthworms, the only other things she has to talk about are harpooning Nan with willow sticks, Oswald Elliot's comic strips, and her step-father's accident. He was killed in the big storm, you know. But since you forbade us from discussing harpooning, earthworms, and comic strips last year, Archibald is in an awkward position. The only thing left for her to talk about is her step-father's untimely accident."

Archibald gasped, laid her head on her desk, and resumed weeping.

Miss Dobbs gripped the yardstick harder. "How about no talking at all," she roared, showing me her molars.

3

Although the day had a rough start, Archibald and me escaped the classroom with no lasting marks, and that was something to celebrate. At three-thirty, when school let out, I threw my arms around Archibald and swung her in the air, not even caring that pristine Eugenia, whose outfit was void of crumbs or crayon marks, was standing too close. Or that one of Archibald's shoes flew off and clipped Eugenia on the side of the head.

Miss Dobbs was out of the classroom, lickety-split. "What's going on out here?"

Archibald pulled away and scowled. "I wasn't doing anything."

Miss Dobbs turned to me.

"Isn't it obvious? I was celebrating. One day over and only a few hundred left."

Selfish Eugenia disturbed my revelry with a moan. She lay on the hallway floor, as blinking and vacant as her two empty-headed cousins. She was a Whitford, through and through.

"That's nothing to celebrate," Miss Dobbs said, dropping to her knees. She pulled a Kleenex from the cuff of her blouse, spit on it, and wiped a scuff mark from Eugenia's face. "Dear heart," Miss Dobbs soothed as she helped Eugenia to her feet before guiding her back into the classroom. "First day and you're set upon by ruffians. Your father, Dr. Whitford, will hear about this. You can be sure of that."

The door closed and Archibald punched me in the stomach for getting her in trouble.

We didn't speak at all as we gathered our things from the cloakroom. The silence was killing me. "Archibald," I finally said. "Do you have your lunch pail?"

Her eyes narrowed. "Do you have yours?"

"I don't think that's the point. Nan arranged for *me* to accompany *you*. That makes me responsible—the accompanier, if you will. All you have to do is tag along. Tagalongs aren't expected to do much except admire the accompanier and do everything they say."

That seemed to irritate Archibald, and she picked up her lunch pail and walloped me. Hitting me was becoming a habit.

"I didn't tell you to do that," I said, rubbing the spot.

"Didn't you?"

I picked up my lunch box and walloped her harder. Now we were even-steven. Even so, I had to fight the urge to give her hair a tug.

We'd hardly made it out of the school door when Archibald's shoulders slumped. She had been holding them tight around her ears for most of the day. Leaning down, she plucked a blade of grass and began chewing on the white root. I did likewise, although it changed my plans. I had envisioned a leisurely Frankenstein-walk home, with Archibald and I grunting affectionately at each other and drooling until our chins were raw. But with our tongues twirling around grass roots, it wouldn't be authentic. So there was no choice but to pretend to be Huck Finn and Tom Sawyer. *They* chewed roots like it was going out of style.

Archibald made the perfect Tom: an uptight little rule-follower. But I didn't tell her that, because people rarely liked to be called uptight. That's when I, as the mischievous Huck Finn, came up with the idea to let the air out of Miss Dobbs' car tires.

"Um, I don't think that's a good idea," Archibald said.

"Of course it's not a good idea. If it were, everybody would do it." I waggled my eyebrows. "That's why it's a *great* idea. Besides, it will make Miss Dobbs think twice before she picks a new favourite."

Archibald looked a bit confused. "How will letting air out of her tires stop her from doing that?"

It was hard not to roll my eyes. "Karma! Everyone knows that. Ditching enamoured children like you who practically drool every time they see her is like gobbing on the baby Jesus. She can't treat you like that and get away with it!"

The look of shock on Archibald's face made me wonder if I'd gone too far. "I don't think Miss Dobbs gobs."

"She doesn't have to, she's a ditcher."

Archibald considered my statement, then began to hem and haw. She was the slowest hemmer and hawer I'd ever met. We were going to be there until doomsday. "New plan," I said, thinking on the fly. "We won't let the air out to get even, we'll let it out so Oswald Elliot can rescue her." Archibald was a romantic at heart, and she wouldn't be able to resist a little matchmaking.

"I'm not sure she wants to be rescued, either."

"We'll never know unless we try. It's like a scientific experiment. And no teacher worth their salt would discourage a student from science."

Archibald wrinkled her nose, so I knew she was warming to the idea. While she warmed, I started on the first tire. After unscrewing the cap, I placed a small stone on the valve. By pressing on the stone I could push down the knobbly thing, letting the air out. I had seen someone do that on the Wonderful World of Disney, a family show for up-and-coming delinquents.

By the time Archibald agreed, my fingers were tiring out. Letting air out of tires was harder than it looked. If Timmy Crybaby-Head hadn't come along, I don't think we'd have ever gotten the job done.

"Whatcha doing?" Timmy Crybaby-Head asked, tilting his melon from side to side.

Archibald and me nearly jumped out of our skins. We were concentrating so hard on what we were doing we'd forgotten to keep watch. As casually as we could, we stood and brushed off our skirts. "What does it look like?"

Timmy shrugged.

"If it doesn't look like we are doing anything, then we're probably not."

"It looks like you're letting the air out of Miss Dobbs' tires."

"Good thing no one takes you seriously," I said.

"Miss Dobbs might."

I could feel Archibald's shoulders rising, and I knew it was only a matter of time before she let out a wail. That would be a dead giveaway. I had to think fast. "The truth is," I said, stepping towards Timmy, "Archibald and me are playing Huck Finn and Tom Sawyer."

Timmy's eyes widened. "Can I play?"

"You could, but all the best parts are taken." I made a line in the gravel with the toe of my shoe. "Archibald is Tom and I'm Huck. Unless you want to be Aunt Polly."

Timmy's face fell. Aunt Polly wasn't enticing enough. "Isn't there anyone else?"

I looked at Archibald, and she shrugged. "Maybe a nonspeaking part," she said.

My eyes lit up. "If you play a nonspeaking part, you can't repeat anything you see or hear."

"Because I can't speak."

"That's right."

Timmy mulled it over for a while. "Okay. Who am I?"

"A tree," I said. "But not just any kind of tree. A tree for climbing and hiding in."

"Where we store our best treasure," Archibald added.

"Can I help let the air out of Miss Dobbs tires?"

I looked him over. "How bendy are your tree limbs?"

Timmy flexed one arm, then the other. I don't think he was coordinated enough to do both at the same time. "Pretty bendy."

Archibald and I looked at each other before nodding.

A smile crossed Timmy's face, from one ear to the other, the same as the day Archibald told him about Miss Dobbs and Oswald Elliot kissing in the car in the parking lot at the Curling Rink. That's when he admitted that sometimes his mom did the same thing with the local mechanic. Then, quick as a flash, Timmy dropped to his knees. He knew what to do without me even telling him. "I've helped my dad let the air out of tires hundreds of times," he said. "Keeps my mom at home."

We had hardly done any more damage before Archibald started complaining about her fingers, saying they were cramping up, and how was she supposed to do well in tomorrow's spelling test with gnarly hands? "Besides," she said, "if we only let out half the air, Miss Dobbs will only be half as angry."

"It doesn't work that way." Timmy stood and brushed off his knees. "My mom loses her mind when dad and me fiddle with her tires. Says half the air is almost as bad as no air at all. And if my dad can't trust her to drive around town by herself, then why did he buy her a car in the first place? Dad says that he didn't buy it for her to have her carburetor calibrated."

Timmy lost me. Nan never talked about having her carburetor calibrated, so I was out of my depth. Even so, I figured Timmy, being a boy, knew what he was talking about.

After we'd let out enough air to be inconvenient—but not enough for Archibald to have a conniption—we settled down in the bushes that skirted the school parking lot. It was the first time since I'd met him that I thought Timmy wasn't that bad, and I was pretty sure he disliked Miss Dobbs as much as I did. How could he not? In first grade, after someone complained about Timmy's persistent pee-smell, she told us to hold our breath whenever he passed. That year, whenever we played dodgeball, Timmy was it; Miss Dobbs said she was toughening him up.

I looked from Timmy to Archibald. They had to admit this was more fun than dodgeball, and that out in the open like this Timmy hardly smelled like pee at all. I poked Archibald in the ribs and grinned. She didn't grin back.

"I'm getting hungry. My mom is going to worry if I'm not home soon."

I poked Timmy, but then he looked like he was going to cry.

"I can't feel my legs anymore."

These two were the worst bunch of bush-crouchers that ever lived. I had to remind Timmy he was a tree, which was a nonspeaking part, unlike the talking-walking trees in *Lord of the Rings*.

"There are talking trees?" Timmy's eyes widened in wonder.

I rolled my eyes. Another mouth-breather who hadn't read the classics. "Yes," I said. "But they all get burned in a fire." My gaze burrowed into Timmy, whose eyes shrunk to normal size. Served him right for wanting to be a talking tree. Besides, when was the last time he played with anyone after school? He was lucky to be a tree. His numb legs aside, he had no idea about hardship. Not until he'd sailed on a sailboat bed alongside Captain Ahab, bleary-eyed and punch drunk from being tossed around on a churning sea. Not until he'd deboned a whale on a sun-baked deck using nothing but his teeth. No, sir. Until he'd looked Old Lady Griggs in at least one of her wonky eyes and not turned into a pillar of salt, he had nothing to complain about.

When Timmy started whining that he had to pee, we hightailed it out of there. He didn't make idle threats. We pretend-hugged Timmy and reminded him he was a *silent* tree before going our separate ways.

Archibald and me grabbed hands. "Let's not be Huck and Tom," she said as soon as we were alone. "Let's just be us."

"That's kind of boring."

"I know. But the real *us* won't get arrested."

I thought of the Happy Valley Penitentiary and my should-have-been parents, the ones who ditched me so Nan had to raise me. I thought of the three of us reunited in matching prison stripes and bold black numbers. They'd be the worst bunk mates. Hogging all the blankets and counting out squares of toilet paper like they were gold. (Nan made me count squares; I was allowed four, but sometimes I wrapped my hand like a mummy when she wasn't looking.) The worst thing, though, would be scraping the answers of my spelling test on the prison cell wall, due to paper cutbacks. Miss Dobbs would refuse to correct it. She was a stickler for writing our answers on a clean piece of foolscap, one that hadn't been stuck to the heel of anyone's shoe when they came back from the bathroom.

Considering all that, I squeezed Archibald's hand, and we began swinging our lunch pails and skipping. On our way home, we climbed trees to check nests. To our disappointment, all were abandoned, it being so late in the season. Archibald rolled over a large stone and squatted to watch the ants panic as they moved their eggs out of harm's way. "That's me on the inside," she said, looking at the hubbub. "I just start to feel safe and then..."

"Someone dies," I completed her thought.

She nodded.

We watched for a while without saying a word. Then I squatted down beside her and pressed my forehead against hers. "I'll help you move your eggs," I whispered.

She pressed her head into mine and nodded before setting down the stone.

There was no arm swinging after that. We walked quietly in the bee-buzzing sunshine, not saying, just knowing. Even my eye blinking felt sad. Being an accompanier was harder than I thought. The heaviness of it pressed into my shoulders.

4

When Archibald's house came into view, my heart grew wings and gave a flutter. Every time one of Archibald's dads died, her mother used the life insurance money to add on another room or two. Her house was a monument to hodgepodge grandness—a place where Frankenstein could walk the halls with impunity, pirouette in the living room, and flip pancakes in the kitchen. I scanned the whole of it and wondered which room Archibald's own dead dad had inspired. I was about to poke her when a sharp voice intruded.

"Girls?"

Archibald stiffened beside me. I could feel my back get up as I looked first to Archibald, then followed the voice to the bloated woman leaning on a veranda railing. She was fanning herself with last week's church bulletin, a broken pair of opera glasses dangling around her neck. I couldn't place her. Hadn't seen her at church, or visiting inmates along the penitentiary fence. Hadn't seen her shuffle down the aisles of Happy Valley Druggist or buy pastries from the Saggy Buns Bakery either. Archibald must have sensed my confusion, because she began spy-talking to me, her lips tight and hardly stirring while she smiled and waved. "That's Mrs. Figgler. She just moved here."

Not another newcomer, I almost said aloud. Happy Valley was becoming awash with strangers. First the extra Whitfords and now this Figgler woman. Mayor Forde would have a fit if he had to change the population number on the Happy Valley welcome sign again. The last time he had a fit, it took three R.C.M.P. officers to corral him in a corner of the Happy Valley Beer Parlor. It made the front page of the Happy Valley Journal: "God-Appointed Mayor Refuses to Acknowledge New Resident."

In the article, Mayor Forde, screaming and flailing as he was dragged out of his favourite drinking establishment, insisted that until a person paid their taxes and voted for him they weren't worth his time. Griggs agreed. She swore she'd never vote for him or pay her taxes if that would keep his big mouth shut. She said it would be Christmas come early.

My eyes scanned the empty cardboard boxes stacked up around Mrs. Figgler and leaning against the walls of her flakey old house before flicking back to her. "For a stranger, she seems awful friendly."

"Awful maybe, but I'm not so sure about friendly. My mom calls her a busybody. Says she's not even unpacked yet and her nose is in everybody's business but her own. Mom hardly has time to sit down and Mrs. Figgler is on the doorbell again, wanting to know who has the best this or who has the best that. Sometimes we hide in the cellar."

I examined Mrs. Figgler. As a busybody, she might give Old Lady Griggs a run for her money. "What does she want?" I asked, without moving my lips.

Archibald shrugged.

"Let's find out."

Archibald was reluctant at first, but I reminded her that I

was the accompanier and she was a tagalong. The reminder didn't seem to please her, but she kept me within lunch pail swinging distance.

We strode towards Mrs. Figgler's picket-fenced yard. No Frankenstein walking, or steps troubled by witches waiting to pounce on us from nearby bushes. *Jesus Loves Me* bubbled on Archibald's lips; singing it made her feel better when she sensed impending doom. And if Mrs. Figgler's bristly face wart wasn't enough to cause concern, the wonky fence that teetered even though there wasn't a breath of wind was. To be honest, we weren't close enough to Mrs. Figgler to see if she had a bristly face wart, but considering the muumuu that hid a body as lumpy as curdled milk, it stood to reason.

With every step we took towards her, she took one towards us. As we ventured into spitting range, Mrs. Figgler's lips tightened and she looked us over, each in turn. "Well, I don't have all day, so let's get down to brass tacks, shall we?" Her eyes narrowed at Archibald. "I was told you'd be with the new Whitford girl. That's why I went to all this effort, putting in my teeth, combing my hair. Doing my best to make a good impression."

"This is your best?" I asked incredulously.

"Don't take that tone with me. I wasn't even talking to you and your seasonal head."

I took a step back.

"That's right, young miss! I know all about your little comic strip and how Oswald Elliot draws you and all your bizarreness. A different head for every occasion. A bit of a show-off, if you ask me."

"Bizarreness isn't a word," I replied haughtily.

"Don't tell me about words. I know words, I have all the best words." Her nostrils flared. "I was expecting Dr. Whitford's daughter. Birds of a feather, as they say."

"We're not birds," Archibald said.

"No, but you and Eugenia are both half-orphaned. This one," she waved a hand at me, "is only abandoned. Not the same thing."

Archibald's nod was almost imperceptible, and I could feel her disappear into herself; an ant hiding her eggs. As much as I wanted to comfort her, I couldn't. I wondered if Archibald would rather be with another orphan and not me.

"Well, let's get this over with." Mrs. Figgler turned and ambled back towards the house.

But I wasn't exactly sure what she wanted us to do. I looked at Archibald; she shrugged her shoulders, and I shrugged mine back. Now I knew why her family hid in the cellar. Mrs. Figgler mumbled as she wove her way through the boxes strewn on the veranda, her muumuu appearing and then disappearing in the debris. With an exaggerated sigh, she lowered herself on a creaky porch swing, her muumuu billowing around her. "Don't be shy, girls," she said, patting the spot beside her. "I've been waiting all afternoon for someone from your household to come scurrying down that path, but the rest of your crew is either deaf or just plain rude."

"My money's on rude," I whispered to Archibald.

"Hurry up." Mrs. Figgler patted the spot again. "I'm not in the mind to chase after you. Besides, I've got cookies."

"Cookies?"

"Yes." She waggled a dish in the air.

I looked from Archibald to Mrs. Figgler. "What's the harm?" I said, pulling Archibald towards the veranda. "Besides," I added, "how often do you get cookies before supper?"

"I only have one cookie," Mrs. Figgler said, correcting her former claim. "I'm not made of money, you know. So you'll have to share."

When I saw what was on the dish, it was hardly worth the effort. It contained a single cookie with a fly buzzing around it. I didn't know if the brown bits were raisins or chocolate chips—or insect droppings. "You can have the cookie," I whispered to Archibald, sweet as can be.

She elbowed me in the ribs.

"I've got some freshly squeezed lemonade too. But you must share a glass." As she poured, she once again instructed us to sit, but I wasn't sure where. The only place amongst the boxes was the creaky porch swing, and from what I could hear, it was already moaning under Mrs. Figgler's weight.

Archibald was the first to take her up on her offer. She grabbed on to the swing's armrest and somehow welded herself to it with one of her wiry arms. She looked like she was on the top end of a teeter-totter. I was impressed. The only place left for me was the flaky spot in the middle. I took my place with a little hesitation. Even with the two of us as a counterbalance, the swing tilted heavily in Mrs. Figgler's direction. I had to link arms with Archibald just so I didn't get absorbed in her flowery muumuu, never to be seen again.

Mrs. Figgler didn't seem to notice our discomfort when she picked up the cookie plate and shook it at us. Archibald scrunched her shoulders and declined. I didn't have that luxury.

"Thank you." I picked up the disappointment with my free hand, flies and all. I waved the cookie through the air to chase off its passengers. "Mmm," I said, unconvincingly. It wouldn't even pass Old Lady Griggs' sloppy inspection. I leaned over and pressed it into Archibald's tight lips.

"Well, let me say this from the start: I'm not one to tell tales." Mrs. Figgler sucked in her nostrils. "Everyone in Moose Mountain, where I used to live, saw me as a pillar of the community. Wept buckets when I left."

I nodded and kept pressing.

"So, I don't think I'm overstepping when I say you two girls are quite the pair. One looks like she's been constructed with spare parts, and the other—well, your stepfathers have the lifespan of a fruit fly." She looked directly at Archibald. "I bet you hardly get used to spelling their last names before they're gone."

Archibald's lips were turning red, but I wasn't sure if it was from Mrs. Figgler's thoughtless comment, or if they were swelling from the cookie I was ramming into them. I stopped the barrage. "Mrs. Figgler, how long have you lived in Happy Valley?"

"A month next Sunday. Why?"

"Just wondering. Has Mrs. Griggs come over with her Welcome Wagon shepherd's pie casserole yet?"

"No, I don't believe she has."

"It must have been an oversight. Everyone who's *anyone* gets one. I'll tell her she must. No one does a shepherd's pie like Old Lady Griggs. The Mayor raves about it. Said so in the Happy Valley Journal."

Mrs. Figgler took a sip of lemonade, mulling over the idea of a free meal.

"Girls! What in God's name are you two doing?" It was Mrs. Willoughby, Archibald's mother, calling to us in a shrill voice from the other side of the gate.

Mrs. Figgler's head snapped in her direction, and her body stiffened with offence. "I asked them to join me."

Mrs. Willoughby gathered herself. "I see that," she said, striding closer. "But now the girls must come home. They've taken up enough of your time."

"Very well, Mrs. Willoughby. I was only being neighbourly."

Archibald slid off the swing first, planting her legs as if we were playing crack the whip. She swung me off quick as you like, saving me from sliding down the length of the swing and being absorbed by Mrs. Figgler's massive muumuu. I wanted to hug her. It was like she'd read my mind and saved me from the great abyss. But as soon as the deed was done, she snatched her hand away and glared.

"Are you mad?" I asked as we reached the front gate.

Archibald said nothing, but I felt the bitterness bubbling from deep inside her. That's when I realized she wasn't playing crack the whip, she was catapulting me. My backbone stiffened. If I wasn't careful she'd leave me in the schoolyard for all the inmates of the Happy Valley Penitentiary to spit sunflower seeds at. I was angry, like the time she'd told me she had her very own comic strip, and Griggs declared it so gripping it was a shoo-in for the Pulitzer surprise.

"Are you mad?" I repeated.

"My lips are pulsing."

"What's the big deal? There's not a circus performer alive that wouldn't kill for pulsing lips. Don't look a gift horse in the mouth." I raised an eyebrow and tried not to look down my nose as I spoke to her. "I wish I could be so lucky as to have pulsing lips."

Archibald turned and faced me. I could almost see them throb, like a thousand bees had been feasting at her pink tulip mouth.

"It was only a bit of cookie dust," I offered. "You must be allergic."

Before Archibald had time to wallop me with her lunch pail, Mrs. Willoughby manhandled us through the front gate like a couple of discombobulated chicks. Her eyes focused over our heads on Mrs. Figgler as if she were Medusa. For her part, Mrs. Figgler looked innocent enough, sitting there all forlorn on the paint-chipped porch swing. No one would ever suspect she served fly-speckled rocks to unsuspecting schoolchildren.

"Thanks for entertaining my girls," Mrs. Willoughby said, although there was no gratitude in her voice.

"Don't mention it." Mrs. Figgler rose from her roost. "I'm

marvelous with children. Haven't had one die on me yet. By the by, I see you've taken to wearing pink. A rather perky colour, considering your last husband's not been dead two months. Would have donned the black a little longer if I were you."

"Well, you're not me, are you?" Mrs. Willoughby took us each in hand and hurried us across the street, leaving Mrs. Figgler to mull over their exchange.

It wasn't until we were well out of earshot that Mrs. Willoughby gave us a thorough going over. She paused on Archibald. "What happened to your lips? Did you get into a fight?"

Archibald narrowed her eyes at me.

"First day jitters," I said, not wanting to get into the cookie incident and Archibald's blatant refusal to be neighbourly.

Archibald mumbled something about taking care of her own ant eggs before she turned on her heel and stomped into the house.

"Never mind her," Mrs. Willoughby said, her gaze following her daughter. "With the baby and Mr. Willoughby's untimely..." she paused. "Well, you know, Archibald just hasn't been herself. But I want to thank you, Celia, for bringing her home from school. She's been dreading the walk home for weeks, because of Mrs. Figgler, and I think you might have made it easier. You make her forget her troubles by getting her into new ones. You're a very good friend, Cclia."

I nodded and let out the sigh I'd been holding in all day, so Mrs. Willoughby would know I was thoroughly exhausted.

5

Last week, when Nan had asked me if I'd like to accompany Archibald home from school on our first day, I was so excited I stopped listening. I saw Nan's lips move, but her words were all mushed together. Something about a bunch of rules and expectations that no one but her cared about. It was like listening to Griggs when she had heatstroke.

"Did you hear me, Celia?"

I dreamy-eyed nodded. My mind was on strolling with Archibald unsupervised. "Archibald and me..."

"Archibald and *I*," Nan interrupted. "We've gone over this umpteen times."

My lips curled. "If I say *Archibald and I*, the words come out of my nose. If I say *Archibald and me*, they come out of my heart."

Nan's eyes softened. "Well, if you're going to butcher the language, that's the perfect reason to do it. For now though, let's go over the rules. The last thing I need is you roaming the streets confirming all of Enid Whitford's proclamations of doom."

Proclamations of doom! What did Mrs. Whitford know? She was all lipstick and nail polish. Doom hadn't touched her since the day she'd cut ties with her deranged sister, Agnes Obermeyer, after she set Mrs. Whitford's hair-sprayed beehive hairdo on fire with her crinkled cigarette. Mrs. Whitford smelled like singed chicken feathers for nearly a week, but Griggs said it was more like the sulphurous stench of Hell.

Looking back, I should have paid attention to Nan's instructions. But how was I to know which of her blatherings were indispensable? Closing my eyes, I tried to remember everything she'd said to me. Was it be careful of witches or that witches were a figment of an overactive imagination? Was it stay on the road or stay *off* the road and skirt through Farmer Hempel's pasture instead? Avoid Mrs. Whitford or make the woman's life miserable? Oh, why did Nan have to be so long-winded?

I surveyed my surroundings. I couldn't go back to Archibald's now, considering the mood she was in, and I refused to hightail it back to school. It was called the Happy Valley School For Reluctant Children for a reason. Besides, Miss Dobbs was likely in the parking lot kicking at her airless car tires. My heart beat double-quick. I'd rather be boiled by witches than run into her again. I could take Main Street, but that was Mrs. Whitford's domain. I'd rather hit myself in the head with a hammer than stroll into her web. She was still harbouring ill feelings about Nan's house auction.

Here's what happened. On the day of the auction, when my should-have-been parents tried to trick Nan out of her house, and Griggs saved the day by beating them at their own game, Mrs. Whitford was happy as a clam, waving her gloved hands through the air as if she owned the place, showing off her brand new red convertible. It wasn't until she found me and Archibald in the back seat that she got testy.

The two of us, Archibald and me, had taken up prime spots

on the pristine red and white leather seat, because it was perfect for keeping an eye on both the auctioneer and my no-good should-have-been parents. To pass the time, we began picking the mud off the bottoms of our bare feet. Once my feet were clean, there was nothing left to do except scratch *Celia was here* with a stick in that soft leather seatback. That must have been what set Mrs. Whitford off. Never saw anything like it. Thought she was going to tear off all her clothes and set herself on fire. Doc Marley had to medicate her. Mr. Whitford said the peace of having a medicated wife almost made the etching worth it—or at least he said it in my head, I'm not sure which. Consequently, I was in no hurry to run into Mrs. Whitford on Main Street. Watching her bring Eugenia into the classroom was about all my poor heart could take for one day.

I would have to brave Farmer Hempel's Herefords, I decided. As long as I didn't run into Wild Roan, the one that lost her mind when Archibald and me and Nan were traipsing across the pasture during the lightning storm that killed her step-father, I was confident I'd survive.

In the full light of day, the pasture looked pleasant enough. The pigs were in their pen near the barn; the chickens were in their coop, and the turkeys were strutting about the yard enclosure. The sheep looked like little white fuzz balls at the far end of the field, all fluffy and delightful. But looks can be deceiving, so I steely-eyed the place on the lookout for witches, for cows that foamed at the mouth, and for Oswald Elliot, who, if he'd finished his sketch, would be up for finding new ways of desecrating my visage.

I skirted along the fenceline and accidentally poked my finger on a barb. Served me right for being an accompanier; I should have known better. I kicked the fence post. That's when my eyes found the spring calves, who'd grown big over the summer. Some frolicked while others sidled up to their dewy-eyed mothers, who blinked and chewed their cud. Behind them, something sleek and majestic stepped into view.

A horse! Right there in the middle of the cow patties. Didn't even know that Farmer Hempel *had* a horse. I hung on the fence for a moment longer, marveling. I'd never been this close to a horse before, and my heart pounded in my chest as I scanned the ground for an offering of friendship. There wasn't much; what farmer Hempel hadn't mowed, greedy cows had devoured. Looking around, I checked to see if there was anyone to stop me. Not a stopper in sight. Maybe that wonderful new beast would be the Samwise Gamgee to my Frodo. My heart leapt at the thought, so I crawled under the barbed wire and stepped into the pasture.

Samwise didn't notice me at first, or for that matter, at all. He grazed as if he didn't have a care in the world. How could I not love him? Picking my way around the cow pies and muddy bits, I kept one eye out for Wild Roan and the bloated earthworms caught in last night's deluge. I was so caught up in my surveillance that I didn't notice how far I'd walked from the barbwire fence and safety. I realized I didn't have a clue which cow Wild Roan was; they all looked the same: red with white faces.

Thinking back to that night we walked from Nan's house to Archibald's, I was so distracted by the witches and lightning storm I didn't get a real good look at which cow charged Oswald Elliot and his intrepid banana bike. She could be any of those brutes casually munching, waiting to impale me on her curly horn.

If Wild Roan stomped me, I didn't stand a chance. "Samwise," I called at the top of my voice. He didn't even raise his head or nicker at me. Already a disappointment. That's when I heard a snort. Out of the corner of my eye, I saw a cow pawing the ground. To be polite, I pawed back; I was rather good at animal talk, a regular Dr. Doolittle. I would have to tell Archibald of my discovery. Maybe we could lie on the ground and wriggle to comfort the earthworms. That's when I got the idea to curtsy. If we could copy the animals, perhaps they could copy us. But the cow didn't even try. She pawed the ground once more before lowering her head and tilting it the same way Archibald and me adjusted our bolty necks. I almost lost my breath. She was going to Frankenstein-walk.

I clasp my hands over my heart at the thought. I curtsied once more, this time deeper, my arm waving in front of me as an extra flourish. The cow, so focused on running at me with her head low and twisted to one side, missed the entire thing. I wasn't sure what to do.

How could she mistake a curtsy? I called for Samwise. He'd know what to do, but he didn't even lift his head. I nickered, I whinnied, and I was just about to bark when a pair of large rough hands snatched me by the arm and hauled me back over to the safe side of the barbwire fence.

"What do you think you're doing?" Farmer Hempel bellowed, his face so close to mine I could see the large pores on his nose were clogged with grain dust.

I shrugged.

"Do you want to get killed? It was bad enough that you and your Nan traipsed through my property during the worse lightning storm of the year, but haranguing my animals for no apparent reason? Well, that's beyond the pale."

His blood was high. I'd never seen Farmer Hempel like that. He was usually chewing the inside of his cheek or pestering Mayor Forde about having a tractor pull. *The crowds we'd draw*, he'd say. *Best thing since sliced bread.* When he was through with his pestering, he'd search out Old Lady Griggs and try to squash her honeymoon hat. Griggs claimed he saved all his flatulations just for her. That made him a wonder to me, almost heroic. But I'd never, in all my seven years, seen him get angry at a child.

"Archibald was there too." I blinked hard, focusing on a pore so blocked it was ready to erupt at any moment. "It was the night her latest step-father died, remember?"

Farmer Hempel straightened and patted the top of my head. "How could I forget?" His voice was forgiving and far away. He shifted, chewed the inside of his cheek, and looked down at me with kinder eyes. "Celia, whatever possessed you to tease my cows?"

"I wasn't teasing them, I promise. I was trying to talk with them, using their own language. Kind of like Jane Goodall does with the chimpanzees. Nan got a book about her out of the library. *My Friends, The Wild Chimpanzees*. Have you read it?"

Farmer Hempel shook his head.

"Oh, it's wonderful. You really should. If Miss Goodall can make friends with some wild chimpanzees, why can't I with a few old smelly cows?"

There was a long pause before Farmer Hempel answered. "Can't argue with you there. But *that* old smelly cow," he pointed to the cow whose ears were pointing straight towards us, "she'll grind you into the ground."

The thought made my stomach do flip-flops. "Why do you keep her?"

"She protects the herd, keeps away the coyotes."

"Does she come after you?"

"Used to when I first got her. She's good with me now." He grimaced. "Remember what she did to Oswald Elliot's bicycle?"

I nodded.

"You wouldn't fare any better."

I scanned the herd. "Is that your only mean one?"

"Tell you the truth, most cows get a little protective after they've had a calf. But as the calves grow, the cows ease off. Wild Roan is different. She's mean all year round. And she'll tell you so. See the way she paws the ground?"

I nodded.

"She's telling you she's going to charge. And notice the way she turns her head and looks at you with one eye? That tells you she means business. Now listen." He paused. "Did you hear that? The snort? She's talking to you just the way Jane Goodall's monkeys talk to her. Except she's talking cow."

Farmer Hempel walked me around the fenceline, pointing out things to watch for. Different kinds of plants, like pigweed that makes the cow's milk taste off, and yarrow, and nettles. And after we'd poked around for a while, I got up enough courage to ask about Samwise.

"Who's Samwise?"

"Your horse."

"Last time I checked, his name was Fade."

"Fade? What kind of name is that?

"The kind my wife gave him."

I rolled my eyes. "Is your wife a reader?"

He rubbed his bristly chin with a burly hand. "That depends if you're comparing her to your Nan. No one in Happy Valley reads as much as that woman."

"Figures." I looked towards Samwise, but he was still ignoring me, not realizing I was his Frodo. "Only an unread person would pick a name like Fade. A reader would scan their memory for every book they'd ever read, and when the right name pulled away from the others, they'd know."

Farmer Hempel gave me a queer look before he escorted me to the end of the driveway. "No shortcuts," he said. "Eventually, that wild old cow will get used to seeing you. Then maybe you can cross the pasture on your own."

"And make friends with Samwise Gamgee?"

"Whoever he is," Farmer Hempel said, before turning to the house.

6

My adventure in Farmer Hempel's field made me want to accompany Archibald home every day. It was the best excuse to practice my Jane Goodall on that wild roan cow. I skipped my way towards Main Street, not caring if I ran into Mrs. Whitford. What could she do anyway? Besides, it would give me a chance to check on my sidewalk stars.

Since my comic strip was such a success, Mayor Forde had commissioned painted sidewalk stars to run down the length of Main Street. Anywhere I'd caused a kerfuffle that Oswald Elliot had dutifully sketched was marked by a star, and maps marking the spots were sold at the Happy Valley Druggist. That way when a newcomer came to town, they could buy a map and snap a picture of themselves re-enacting whatever I'd done at the appropriate spot. Nan thought it was a dirty business and refused to sell the maps whenever she worked at the druggist's. I didn't blame her. None of the stars were hers.

It wasn't till I had passed Saggy Buns Bakery that I spotted them. Not the stars, they were hidden by the throngs of people gawking. I spotted Miss Dobbs and Oswald Elliot. Those two hadn't been seen out together in public since Archibald caught them in the curling rink parking lot, steaming up Miss Dobbs' car windows. Now Miss Dobbs was steaming up the street with her yelling. Folks had stopped to stare.

For safety reasons, I scanned for Mrs. Whitford. She was standing outside the drugstore, slack-jawed, and so engrossed with the comedy of errors, she didn't even notice her sister was a stone's throw away. Her husband and another man, most likely Mr. Whitford's brother, the new doctor in town, were on ladders hanging up a new sign above the one that said *Happy Valley Druggist*. In big red letters, it stated, *Dr. Whitford: I'll Only Touch You When I Have To*.

"His office is going to be above the drugstore," said Agnes Obermeyer, who had quietly sidled up to me.

"Whose?" I said.

"Dr. Whitford's, of course. And let me tell you, Doc Marley will not take this lying down. He's in a real flap. Said he's been bringing hands-on medicine to this town for years. And he doesn't think an upstart like Whitford should stick his nose in where it doesn't belong." She paused and gave a little grunt. "But then again, that's the same policy his brother has with my sister. It's the Whitford way."

Agnes leaned against the nearest lamppost, wearing her fuzzy purple bedroom slippers, a crinkled cigarette stuck to her chapped lips. Her hands were shaking, and I wasn't sure if it was because she was standing so close to her sister—endangering her life—or from the thrill of seeing Oswald Elliot cower in Miss Dobbs' presence. Whatever the cause, she was so shaky she offered me a quarter to light her cigarette for her.

I was excited too. Only on a couple of occasions had I seen Miss Dobbs outside of the classroom. But now she was standing in the middle of Main Street, shaking a finger in Oswald Elliot's face. "Don't tell me you didn't let the air out," she bellowed. "I saw you peeking at me through my classroom windows."

Oswald Elliot fumbled with his sketchbook, his gaze burrowed into the ground. "I was watching the girls," he said.

There was a gasp in the crowd. The men on the ladders stilled, looking down at the couple, and Mrs. Whitford's jaw dropped even lower.

"That's worse!" Miss Dobbs shrieked, looking madder than I'd ever seen her. "Someone your age ogling children! Disgusting!"

Oswald Elliot's head snapped up. "For my newspaper comic strip," he said, as if she'd gone daft. "What do you take me for?"

The crowd let out a communal sigh of relief.

But Miss Dobbs was not having it. "I take you for a man desperate enough to deflate my car tires and then try to come to my rescue with your bicycle pump."

"I wasn't coming to your rescue, I was being a good Samaritan."

"You can take your good Samaritan and stick it where the sun don't shine." Miss Dobbs jabbed him in the chest with a bony finger, almost knocking him to the ground. Oswald said something I couldn't hear, and Miss Dobbs jabbed him again.

Agnes Obermeyer puffed on her cigarette. "Where has all their back alley love gone? It makes me shake my head."

Miss Dobbs glanced up to where Mr. Whitford and his brother were hanging the sign and batted her glued-on eyelashes.

"That's where it's gone," I said, as me and Agnes Obermeyer followed Miss Dobbs' gaze towards Mr. Whitford and his newly widowed brother.

"If you're right, Oswald Elliot doesn't stand a chance. Poor bugger."

Agnes was right, and I'd have to tell Archibald. It was news I could whisper to her while Eugenia recycled the air in her empty head. Before turning from the Main Street showdown, I pressed my luck. I came so close to Mrs. Whitford I could have licked her without her knowing. But I stuck out my tongue instead. The rest of the way home, my steps were lighter.

Nan and Old Lady Griggs were having tea when I skipped up the path. I could hear them arguing through the open kitchen window. "I don't care what you say, Molly Canterberry. Mr. Griggs and I bought this house fair and square. Or have you forgotten?"

"Oh, I remember all right."

"Audrey gave me no choice and you know it. It was Celia or the house. What was I supposed to do?"

"You're asking for my advice now? That's rich!"

"I'm not asking for anything."

Nan paused, and I knew she was trying to control herself. "And what did my home cost you? A couple of old buttons. My parents worked a lifetime for this house. They sweated and slaved for it."

"No use getting cross about it now. You agreed to the arrangement. Audrey got the house when she and the no-good-layabout she runs with signed over guardianship of Celia to you, and she tried to sell it for a profit. Not my problem I made the most creative bid. Seemed like a fair trade then, so you can't cry sour grapes now."

I heard a bang, and I guessed Nan had slammed a fist on the chrome table. "I'm not crying anything, Dorigen. But even you have to agree, two buttons aren't a proper bid."

"If it weren't for those buttons, you might be renting from the Whitfords! How would you like them apples?"

Nan didn't say anything to that.

"And you know full well they were more than a couple of old buttons."

There was a long silence, giving me a chance to cross the lawn and press my cheek against the patched mesh on the screen door. I hadn't done that since I caught my should-have-been parents rummaging through Nan's things. My heart was beating as hard as it had back then. I could hardly breathe.

"And need I remind you about Mr. Griggs' eyesight, or lack of it?"

I knew Nan was mulling over her answer. Mrs. Griggs was touchy when it came to her husband. Ever since Mr. Griggs had been buried in the Happy Valley Graveyard, Mrs. Griggs kept a life-size effigy of him propped up at her kitchen table. At times, she dragged him out in public, but mostly he just sat in a chrome chair, his nylon stuffed head lolling to one side. Nan knew not to mention the obvious—that he was dead—so she stuck with the buttons. "They were *buttons*. I don't know how many times I have to go over this with you. They were not real eyes. And if you'd let me, we could go through my sewing box now and find a matching set to replace them."

"You think I'm daft? I know they're buttons! But it's the *meaning* of the thing. Lucky for you, the auctioneer was an idealist, taking sentimental gestures for bids. My husband gave up his button-eyed sight for you. Now every time I look at him, I see those sad little threads run down his cheeks like a trail of tears. Every time I serve him coffee. Every time I dab at his chin with a napkin. His sunglasses do little to hide the sacrifice. Most days I can barely talk of it."

I heard a chair scrape across the floor. "I appreciate all you've done," Nan said, in a tone that I'd heard before. She was patting Griggs on the shoulder. She did the same when she used that tone with me. It was as if she wanted to hypnotize me into thinking something was my idea, like cleaning my room or wearing my clothes the right way out. "But I think charging me rent to live in my own home is going a little too far."

I opened the screen door and stepped into the porch. I needed to see, not just listen. Griggs went on as if she hadn't even heard the squeak.

"You know as well as I that Mr. Griggs has never been a whiz with money." She gave Nan a knowing look as she tapped her palm.

"A fool and his money are easily parted," Nan murmured, her lips hardly moving as she counted out three twenty-dollar bills.

"What's that, Molly?" But Griggs' eyes were on the cash. Without waiting for a response, she rolled up the bills and stuck them in her bra strap. "So," she continued, "when the opportunity came for us to purchase this rundown abode, we jumped at it."

Nan's lips tightened and I could tell by the vein that pulsed at her temple she was boiling mad. Griggs didn't notice. She was too busy checking for creaky floor boards and opening and closing cupboard doors. "And need I remind you it's not your home, at least not anymore. I have the papers to prove it."

7

Nan slammed around the kitchen until suppertime. "Not my home. Papers to prove it. Who does that woman think she is?"

I shrugged.

"Should have never agreed to the auction. But what else was I to do? They had me over a barrel." Nan slammed a few more pots before she turned to me. "Celia," she said, calming herself with a few deep breaths, "how was your first day of grade two?"

I was almost afraid to answer, and I certainly wasn't brazen enough to shrug. Besides, it was a loaded question. I couldn't tell her about Archibald falling apart when Miss Dobbs asked about our summer holidays. Or that Timmy Crybaby Head had almost peed, he was so excited. Miss Dobbs had taken out the mop and leaned it against the side of Timmy's desk, preparing for the deluge. I knew hearing about the whole thing would infuriate Nan. She already had it in for Miss Dobbs.

I couldn't tell her about letting the air out of Miss Dobbs' tires, either. Nan might call me incorrigible. Meeting Archibald's new neighbour was a possibility, though. I didn't think Nan had met her yet. But then I remembered she was a busybody, and Nan disliked busybodies. Mrs. Figgler looked like the type to slither up to Mrs. Whitford, become a member of the Ladies of the Perpetual Indigence Society, Mrs. Whitford's select group of cohorts, and look down on Nan. Nan called them the PIS ladies behind their backs. Frankly, I found the acronym a bit vulgar. With that group, Mrs. Figgler would have all the help she needed to cause trouble, but for whom I didn't know. Yet, I decided to risk it, sort of. "Archibald has an annoying new neighbour."

Nan's forehead crinkled. "Tell her to join the club. I asked about your first day of school, not Archibald's neighbour."

I thought some more. If I told Nan I almost got trampled by Mr. Hempel's cow, she'd only get cross and tell me I had no business trespassing. So I decided on something dependable, something that would make her eyes glaze over and wish she'd never asked the question. "Timmy Crybaby-Head sucked his thumb all recess, which seemed to please Miss Dobbs. She said if he stayed calm he probably wouldn't piddle and it would save her the price of a perfectly good pair of hose."

Nan frowned. "That doesn't sound very exciting."

"We got a new girl."

Nan perked up. "Is she nice?"

I wrinkled my nose. Talking about a Whitford would only lead to trouble, so I changed the subject. "And we had a practice spelling test. Archibald misspelled *because*." I could hear the disappointment in my voice. "Sometimes I wonder why we're friends."

Nan told me to set the table, so I pulled open the silverware drawer.

"You know," she said, "not everyone finds spelling as easy as you."

"Not everyone is my best friend, either." I counted out two of everything. Forks, spoons, and knives.

"Ok smarty pants, let's give this a whirl." She wiped her hands on her apron as she looked up at the ceiling. She was getting ready to play the dictionary game. "Have you ever met a fishwife?"

I had to be careful how I answered. I couldn't actually use someone's name, or Nan would quit playing and send me to my room for being rude. She accepted synonyms only. "I don't think so. Crones are so hard to come by."

Nan raised an eyebrow and smiled. "Well, this hellcat is pretty common."

"Like the shrew down the way?" I asked, wondering if my hairy little toes were crossing the line. But Nan didn't seem to care. We were playing the dictionary game and had just made it past round two.

"I have to admit that one is a bit of a harpy."

I bit my lip and tried to recall all the words Nan called Griggs under her breath. We'd already used the regulars—hellcat, harpy, fishwife, crone and shrew—but there were more, though none came to mind. So I turned my attention to Mrs. Whitford. Nan always had a few doozies for her. "She's not as much of a battleaxe as her mother," I said, grinning.

Nan was almost coming out of her skin with the joy of it. Her hours of reading to me were finally paying off. "In that family, scolds are a dime a dozen."

I tapped my chin, droplets of sweat beading on my brow. She had me; I set down the cutlery and went to retrieve the dictionary. Maybe next time, I'd best the old hag.

"HAG!" I screamed triumphantly.

Nan cackled with delight.

8

Archibald and me spent the next few days at school sweating, waiting for Miss Dobbs to swing her yardstick and yell, *You. It was the three of you. I can feel it in my bones. I thought it was Oswald who let the air out of my tires!* Then she'd pause and place the back of her hand on her forehead, never finishing her statement.

Luckily, Timmy Crybaby-Head was oblivious to the dilemma. His whimpering would have been a dead giveaway. Besides, with all his dribbling he didn't have enough bodily fluid to waste on such luxuries as sweating. But Miss Dobbs never blamed us. She didn't even raise a questioning eyebrow in our direction. She was too busy making sure Eugenia Whitford felt welcome. She even baked her muffins.

"She never baked me muffins," Archibald complained.

"She hasn't swatted you with a yardstick either," I said, a little perturbed. "Last year, when I was ducking right and left, I didn't hear you complain about all the attention I was getting."

Archibald shrugged.

She needed to know the Miss Dobbs I knew. "At least we know she's not a crackerjack witch," I whispered in Archibald's ear. We were watching Miss Dobbs dust Eugenia's cheek free of muffin crumbs. "A *good* witch would have sussed us out in her sleep. She would have known who'd let the air out of her tires by looking deep into her crystal ball before making voodoo dolls of us to slam in her desk drawer. But Miss Dobbs isn't just an incompetent witch, she's a terrible person to boot."

Archibald's head bobbed slightly in the universal sign of defeat. Miss Dobbs must have sensed our commiserating, because when she raised her gaze her eyes flashed. "It's time for USSR," she snapped.

We all looked at each other and blinked. No one knew what USSR was, except for maybe me. It sounded like something I'd overheard Nan and Griggs talk about at the kitchen table. Nan was going on about the war and Mr. Douglas, and how it left him with a limp—just like the guy who wrestled an angel on a set of stairs—only Mr. Douglas' limp was on the inside. Griggs put her hand on her throat and narrowed her eyes. "Those Bolsheviks," she said. Nan told her she was confusing her regimes, but Griggs said it didn't matter. That it was the tone of voice that conveyed the sentiment, not the words that crammed the empty spaces.

With all the wisdom of Griggs, I filled in the blanks. "That's something Mussolini used to do," I said, without raising my hand.

Miss Dobbs' lip twitched. "Really? Mussolini? I doubt you know who the man was."

"He's the guy who," I thought for a moment and decided on what words to use. There were many in my arsenal, because Nan and me had been playing the dictionary game for years. "He's the guy who implemented USSR on the plains of Bulgaria. Growing up as a shepherd, it helped him pass the long lonely evenings when his fingers got too tired from playing the lute. Also, his mother was a shrew. Occam's razor."

"Wrong, wrong, wrong!" Miss Dobbs had gone from a twitching lip to full body spasms. "How many times have I told you to raise your hand?"

I shrugged. To be honest, I'd lost count. Besides, when I raised my hand, she never called on me.

She clip-clopped closer, smacking her yardstick in her palm with every step. Archibald shrunk in her desk, her shoulders up around her ears. I wanted to reach out and comfort her, to tell her that Miss Dobbs had already been cautioned for going through too many yardsticks last year and that this year her swing would be restrained, but it didn't seem Archibald would find much comfort, no matter how many words I crammed in. Miss Dobbs' steps halted as she came alongside my desk. "USSR was not implemented by Mussolini. It has nothing to do with sheepherding or lute playing. It stands for Uninterrupted Sustained Silent Reading. Any fool knows that."

That was the stupidest thing I'd ever heard, and I told her so. "How can you read anything without poking the person in front of you to talk about the exciting parts? Poking keeps me from coming out of my skin, from squealing with delight and weeping with despair."

"Read," she bellowed, slapping a reader down on my desk. "You will be hard pressed to find a passage in *See Spot Run* that will make you squeal with delight or weep from despair."

I flipped through the pages. The pictures were bright enough, but there was no pushing or hair pulling, nothing to make the story feel alive. Nan would not approve. I suspected she'd rather pull out her toenails than read me this drivel.

See Spot Run was nothing like *Jane Eyre*, the book Nan was reading to me now. At recess, Archibald and me re-enacted the scenes. I was Jane and Archibald was my best friend Helen Burns, except Archibald's Helen didn't have to get sick and die; she got pasty and fainted if she got too much sun. If things kept going as they were, soon Archibald would have to agree with me that Miss Dobbs was the epitome of Miss Scatcherd. I slipped down in my seat and kept all my comments about the merits of USSR to myself.

As we read, Miss Dobbs paced the length of windows that covered the west wall of the classroom, slapping the yardstick down in her open palm with each pass. She was waiting for an Oswald Elliot sighting. Waiting for his pointy head to rise over the window ledge so she could whack the casing with the stick and scare the bejesus out of him. I don't know how much reading got done that morning, but Miss Dobbs had to go to the supply cupboard three times to mop the dribbles around Timmy Crybaby-Head's desk.

At recess, I slipped my arm into Archibald's. "Hello, Helen," I said.

"Who's Helen?"

My eyes brightened. "She's Jane Eyre's best friend, just like you're mine. I've told you that before. And they have a horrible teacher, Miss Scatcherd. She could be Miss Dobbs' twin."

Archibald ignored all the important bits. "Does this Helen have warts?"

"No."

"Does she throw harpoons at your Nan?"

I sighed. Archibald was wasting our play time on ridiculous questions. "No, and if you read more, you'd know that."

Archibald blinked hard. "Your Nan reads those books to you. There is only one of you. My mom doesn't have time. There are six of us." She said it as if reading was something that only silly people did. Something people with busy lives found frivolous and a waste of time.

I could feel the heat in my cheeks. Nan didn't lollygag around the house all day, dividing her time between tweezing her nose hairs and examining the flight patterns of migrating birds. "Reading, I'll have you know, is one of our favourite pastimes."

"Good for you." Archibald rose on her tiptoes.

I didn't know what to say, so I leaned over and gave her hair a tug. She tugged mine back. "Helen would never do that," I shouted.

"Neither would Jane," she shouted back.

"How would you know? You've never read the book."

"Because Helen wouldn't be friends with a hair-puller."

She had a point.

After recess, we filed into Miss Dobbs' room like a line of baby ducks. Miss Dobbs continued to clomp back and forth in front of the classroom windows, ready to whack Oswald Elliot.

"Oh, boy," I said, as I took my seat. "More USSR."

Archibald sniffed. She was harboring bitterness.

"Take out your mathematics books," Miss Dobbs said, without turning to look at us. "It's time for USSM. And before you blurt out some ridiculous comment, Celia Canterberry, it's Uninterrupted Sustained Silent Mathematics. And it has nothing to do with Mussolini!"

I nodded. "Mussolini was a reader, not a numbers man." I wanted to add that everyone knew that already, but Miss Dobbs was bearing down on me, and I didn't want to stir the pot. "You're scaring Eugenia."

Miss Dobbs froze.

"No, she's not." Eugenia turned in her seat. Her voice filled the room with all the sweetness of spring lilacs on a dainty breeze.

I made a gagging sound as Miss Dobbs handed Eugenia another muffin.

Archibald had had enough; I could see it by the way she trembled. I leaned forward and placed my hand on her shoulder. "Oh, sweet Helen." She pressed her cheek into my palm, and I knew all was forgiven.

By the next recess Archibald and me were arm in arm again. We skipped out into the sunshine, ignoring Helen's aversion to the heat. That's when we spotted Timmy Crybaby-Head. He was off by himself playing with dead flies. We sauntered in his direction.

"What was all the dribbling about?" I asked, hands on hips.

Timmy shrugged. "Think we'll have USSR after the bell?"

"I don't know."

"There are too many words in that book."

I raised my eyebrows. We couldn't have been reading the same book. "Dick and Jane?"

Timmy nodded.

Life was going to be hard for that boy.

9

I took it upon myself to accompany Archibald home without being asked. Outside Miss Dobbs' classroom, I waited for her to gather her things before I told her the good news.

"You don't have to," she said, her lips tight.

"Jane wouldn't have it any other way."

Archibald grunted. "I don't want to stop at Mrs. Figgler's."

"Good. Neither do I."

"Even if she offers fresh lemonade and cookies?"

I paused at that one. Offerings like that didn't come often, and to be honest, I didn't know if I'd change my mind when the time came. But then I looked at Archibald's top lip. It was still a little pudgy on one side, so my decision was made. I'd forgo my social obligations. "Even then," I said, squeezing her hand.

We arm-swung our way down the shortcut that led to Archibald's house. "Helen," I said. "Don't you think Miss Scatcherd was horrid today?"

Archibald stopped mid-swing. "Who's Miss Scatcherd?"

"Miss Scatcherd is Jane's and Helen's most hated teacher. I already told you that."

"Oh, yeah."

"She's particularly mean to Helen. Jabs her in the chin and ridicules her in front of everyone."

Archibald's eyes grew enormous.

"Just like Miss Dobbs does. First she picks a new favourite and then insists that you talk about your dead dads on the first day of school. You hadn't even had time to catch your breath." I took Archibald's hands in both of mine. "Not even Miss Scatcherd is that brazen. That's why Jane and Helen need each other, just like you need me."

"You need me too."

I leaned over and kissed her on the cheek. Then, making my voice drip like melting butter, said, "That's true, but you need me more."

Archibald mulled my words over for a while, and I knew she was thinking about pulling my hair. I don't know for sure what stopped her, but my money was on Mrs. Figgler. Any child in their right mind wouldn't want to go near that woman on their own, and I was the perfect shield.

We started arm swinging again, but this time harder and with greater joy. Just like Jane and Helen before Helen got deathly sick, though I wouldn't tell Archibald that and spoil the moment. We'd almost made it past Mrs. Figgler's house when I heard the screen door bang and Mrs. Figgler bellow, "There you are, girls." She was waving a dish towel through the air. "I baked a fresh batch of cookies and was hoping I could tempt you with a few."

I pulled Archibald to a stop. Fresh cookies were one of Jane's favourite things. And even though I'd promised Helen I wouldn't partake, it was tearing me apart inside to refuse. "St. John Rivers warned me of this," I said, my knees feigning a buckle. "Only Satan and Lutherans tempt innocent children."

"I'm no Lutheran." The shock of the accusation caused Mrs.

Figgler to tip the chipped plate she was holding, spilling the cookies onto the veranda.

"Well, there you have it." I did a slight curtsy, and Archibald and me skipped the rest of the way to Archibald's house. Neither of us dared a backward glance, but I was sure I could feel Mrs. Figgler's brimstone stare burrowing into me. Nan would probably have to mend a hole in the back of my shirt. "Land sakes, how did this happen?" she'd say. "Science," I'd say. "It's what happens when an unfulfilled Figgler looks at you. Unfulfilled because no one will eat her cookies or drink her lemonade." When I thought of it that way, I almost felt sorry for the old bat.

"I have to show you something," Archibald said, as soon as we stepped inside her house. Her eyes were closed, and she had one hand over her heart, as if waiting for it to slow. When her eyes opened they were steely, unlike the Archibald eyes I was used to. They stopped me in my tracks. They were eyes that had crossed the Rubicon, done the dance of the seven veils, and played Russian roulette with real Russians. It made me wonder if Jane was an excellent judge of character.

Archibald looked down the hallway that separated the porch from the kitchen. Her mother was on the phone and hadn't even noticed us come in, while her brothers, Grenway, Bose, Buttons, and Earl were seated at the kitchen table having an afternoon snack. The baby, Sly, was bouncing on his mother's hip while she tried to talk. We tiptoed past, keeping to the dark side of the hallway. I couldn't understand why Archibald was being so secretive. Usually she barged into the house, calling for her mother as soon as she crossed the threshold. I loved that Archibald, but this one I wasn't so sure about.

That's when I saw them. The grandest doors that were ever made. "They're from an old church in Spain," Archibald said, running a hand over the grain. "Part of my mom's latest addition."

"They look like storybook doors," I whispered.

"I know." Archibald went to turn the knob, but I stopped her. Every tale Nan had ever read me waited behind those doors. All the twists and turns of the carved panels shouted it. More than that, there were two knockers, one for each door. A pair of brass hands holding brass apples. I could have stared at those doors all day. How could Archibald live with such loveliness and not burst from the excitement of it all? Nan wouldn't be able to drag me away from them. In the moonlight, I'd slip notes under them, addressed in sparkly penmanship to all my fairy friends.

"This isn't even what I wanted to show you," Archibald whispered.

"What could be better?"

"You'll see." Archibald turned the knob and slipped through the opening, and I followed her.

The room she led me into was not finished. Old bookshelves from some ancient country were stacked against one wall, piles of books and papers waited for someone to put them in their place, and paint cans and drop cloths were strewn around the room. But even in all of its unfinished clutter, I was astonished. "I don't remember seeing this room on the night of the big storm."

"It was here," Archibald sighed. "Couldn't see it in the dark, and in the morning I didn't have it in me to show you."

I closed my eyes and tried to sniff out threads of Mr. Rochester's pipe tobacco. I wanted to fall on the floor and weep in the wonder of it all. How could Archibald care about Miss Dobbs finding a new favourite when she had this room to come home to?

"So, what's it going to be when it's finished?" I asked.

"A library, of course!" Archibald sounded indignant.

"Oh, I wasn't sure, since your family aren't readers. Thought maybe it would be a solarium or a study."

"What's a solarium?"

I shrugged. My job was to remember the words and spell them properly, after that they weren't my responsibility. Archibald led me deeper into the chaos. "Griggs keeps a pile of books by her bed instead of a bedside table," I said, indicating the tomes piled haphazardly. "She said tables are just a bunch of work. Everyone expects you to dust a table, but only an imbecile would dust books."

Archibald frowned and put a finger to her lips. "Swear that you'll tell no one."

"About a library? You want me to swear that I've never been in your library?"

She nodded.

"Your mom doesn't want anyone to know she reads?"

Archibald's lips went tight, and I knew if I didn't swear her stupid promise we wouldn't take another step. "Okay," I said. "Nobody would believe me, anyway." I crossed my heart and hoped to die if I ever told anyone of her secret library, her *lair*.

Archibald looked even more impressed with the place. "I never thought of it as a lair before, but it kind of is."

We kept on inching forward until it got on my nerves. I tapped Archibald on the shoulder. "Why are we skulking?"

"Don't want to knock over any of the piles. The noise will give us away."

That was good enough for me. It would give me a chance to practice my Hercule Poirot by wiggling my waxed moustache and walking behind Archibald like a duck. I rose on my tiptoes, crunched to my haunches and waded through what seemed like endless stacks of books and papers. It was a waste of money, as far as I was concerned, having a room like this but no one to brag about it to. I rose on my toes once more for good measure. That's when Archibald abruptly stopped and I bumped into her. "Archibald," I said, more annoyed with her than usual. "Need I remind you we're skulking?"

She raised a hand and pointed. "Not anymore."

Across from us, on a fieldstone fireplace mantel, sat the most unusual clock. Once I saw it, I wanted to touch it, but I didn't dare. It was more than a clock — it was one of the Seven Wonders of the World. It was magic. It was what the great doors were protecting. At first I couldn't say anything. I stared without blinking.

"My last dad ordered it for my mom from Prague," Archibald said into the silence.

"Who's Prague?" I asked, taking a step closer.

"Prague's not a person, silly. It's a place."

"Oh."

"It's inspired by the Prague Astronomical Clock," Archibald said, her neck stiff as if she were giving a book report. "There are four figures flanking the clock. Vanity is represented by the figure in the short green robe admiring himself in the mirror. Next is the Miser. He is represented by the greedy man holding a bag of gold. Lust, the love of earthly pleasures, holds the lute. And last but not least, Death is represented by the skeleton who on the hour rings his bell, warning that he could come at any time. As he rings, Lust, Vanity, and the Miser shake their heads, indicating they are not ready to go."

I looked from Archibald to the clock. "How long have you been practicing that little spiel?"

She shrugged. "Ever since my mom unpacked it and I looked it up in the World Book Encyclopedia. But my mom won't let me recite it anymore. She's sick of hearing it, and she said it's no one else's business. She says it was a private gift. Between her and him. And she's afraid that if Oswald Elliot catches wind of it, he'll cheapen it. Make it appear foolhardy. She says that it's the best thing a man has ever given her, besides her children, and she put it in the room inspired by one of her favourite husbands."

"Who's her favourite husband?"

"She won't say."

I looked around. "Which one inspired this room?"

"My dad. Earl's dad inspired the porch."

With a careful step, I was up on the hearth. I didn't even reach up and try to touch the clock. It was too incredible. "Oswald Elliot could never make something so magnificent foolhardy. If he drew it, he'd win the Pulitzer surprise for sure."

Archibald let out a deep breath and stepped up on the hearth beside me. "I know. I wanted to show you, but my mom said I couldn't. She was afraid you'd blab about it to Mrs. Griggs, and that would be almost as bad as Oswald Elliot."

"Why would I blab to Old Lady Griggs?" I could feel my cheeks grow hot. Griggs had been the first person I'd thought about when I saw the clock. The skeleton could be her twin.

"Oh, I didn't think you'd tell her on purpose." She squeezed my hand. "I thought she'd smell the secret and ring it out of you. But now that you're Jane and I'm Helen..."

"There can be no secrets."

Archibald nodded.

The two of us stood there watching the clock, our necks craned in awe. And when it chimed on the hour, and the skeleton rang his bell, and Lust, Vanity and the Miser shook their heads, I got chills.

10

All the way to Farmer Hempel's, I treasured my new secret and vowed I'd take it to the grave. Archibald and me now had an *uncommon knowing*, like the witches in the Salem witch trials. To the witches it was just forest herbs and healing mushrooms, but to the men in black hats it was a reason to light matches. And a knowing like that couldn't be talked about at Nan's kitchen table. It would demean the knowers and the clock from Prague.

When I'd asked Archibald why her last father would give her mother such a clock, she said, "Well, he thought it would bring her comfort. He told her he never gave into lust, greed or worldly pleasures, so he wouldn't need to shake his head when death rang his bell. He'd be safe."

"It didn't work," I observed wryly. I'd always wanted to do that.

"Nothing does." Archibald climbed down from the mantel and pulled one of the World Books from the pile. "Here," she said, pointing to a picture of the Prague clock. "This is its larger twin."

I looked from the fireplace mantel to the World Book. "Words fail me," was all I could think to say.

The whole clock thing got me thinking. If Skeleton rang his bell for me, would I shake my head no, or stand stock-still and let him take me away without a fight? It made me sad just thinking about it.

How many other things didn't I know about? Nan read to me all the time, but just made-up stories. Things old men dreamt up when they had nothing better to do. Plus Charlotte Brontë. But never once did she read The World Book Encyclopedia to me, and that, I had discovered, contained information I could use to make other people feel stupid.

Archibald would know all kinds of things with those books. No one would give a fat Figgler that she couldn't spell. Kids would gather around the teeter-totter, their jaws unhinged, as Archibald blew out her cheeks at the wonder of herself. Captain Ahab and me would have to sharpen sticks on our own. Poke the convicts at the penitentiary fence and tell them about the girl that was too big for her britches. The girl who spent her days showing up their kin. It would kill me to do it, but what choice would I have?

When I reached the farmyard, there was no one in sight, so I wasn't even tempted to spill my guts. The pasture had the usual cows milling around, all willy-nilly, like they didn't have a care in the world, and Samwise Gamgee was still ignoring me when I called to him from my side of the barbwire fence. I called, I sang, I cajoled. And what did I get? Nothing. That Sam was getting on my nerves. "You made a promise to Gandalf," I cried, grabbing hold of the wire fence, narrowly missing the barbs. But Sam didn't even flick an ear in my direction. Did he not remember who Gandalf was? The power he had in his staff? I shook my head sadly. That horse was taking his life into his own hands.

Turning from Samwise, I spied the farmyard. Not a farmer in sight. A perfect time to go exploring. That's when I noticed a plank missing from the side of the barn. The building was old and tilted to one side, and I'd once heard Farmer Hempel tell Nan that his father had built it, and it pained him to see it fall into disrepair. Nan asked him why he didn't repair it. He moved his toothpick from one side of his mouth to the other and said it didn't pain him that much.

I skirted the fenceline, pausing at each fencepost to re-evaluate the situation. Luck was mostly on my side; my sweater only got caught twice on barbs when skirting too close. When I reached the barn, I took a deep breath before sticking my head through the gap between the planks. It took a while for my eyes to adjust, but as soon as they focused, I realized the only thing that stood between me and the barn stall was a manger. And in that manger there was an old tabby cat nursing her late-summer kittens. I slipped through the void as quick as you like and squatted in the manger beside her. The kittens kneaded and purred, all pleased with themselves, and their mother, just as pleased, purred back. It was all I could do to keep myself from pocketing one of those fur balls, but I knew Nan had enough to worry about and didn't need one more mouth to feed.

I continued to sit in that musty old manger, even when my legs cramped. They'll go numb soon, I told myself. That's when I sang *La Traviata*, Nan's favourite opera. If that melodrama didn't make my blood run, nothing would. I was in the middle of the second verse, same as the first, when Farmer Hempel came running around the side of the stall with a shovel raised above his head. He stopped short when he saw me. "Thought the dog was killing the kittens," he stammered.

"I was singing to them," I said, as Farmer Hempel lowered his shovel. "La Traviata."

He stepped closer and looked into the manger. The kittens were still kneading and purring. A puzzled look crossed his face. "Can you sing that last bit again?"

I'd barely gotten out the first few notes when he held up a hand. "That's the sound," he said. "Does your Nan let you sing at home?"

"Not as much as I'd like. And Old Lady Griggs said that my singing doesn't go with our pot and pan band."

Farmer Hempel bit his lip. "A word to the wise. Careful where you belt out that tune, girly. If you don't get shot by a neighbour, one of my critters is liable to put you out of your misery."

11

Nan winked at me as I opened the screen door and skipped inside. She had just got home from her job at the Happy Valley Druggist and was hanging her apron on a peg inside the porch closet. "Look who the cat dragged in."

My feet stuck in their tracks. "Did Farmer Hempel call you?"

"No, why?"

I shrugged, glad that he didn't tell her I half killed his kittens with my singing. "A cat is a farm animal, isn't it?"

"I suppose." Nan looked me up and down. "For now though, my little Carolus Linnaeus, change into your everyday clothes and let's head out to the garden. Our potatoes need tending."

"Potatoes," I said, trudging up the stairs. "Who cares about potatoes?"

I peeled off my school clothes and threw them on the floor. They were supposed to be hung up if clean and put in the laundry if dirty. Most days I got it wrong, so *why bother?* was my philosophy. Nan would look at my laundry pile and furrow her brow. "What's wrong with this?" I'd shrug. She'd go to the closet and pull out a shirt I'd hung up by the arm hole. "Didn't you see this lump of jam?"

I'd shrug again. "Thought I'd suck on it during my next spelling test. Lumps of jam are lucky."

Unfortunately for me, Nan wasn't superstitious.

Peering under my sailboat bed, I searched for my everyday clothes. Captain Ahab liked to swaddle his stump in them when I was away. They were a twisted heap in the corner. "Some people," I muttered, putting on the wrinkled mess.

The thought of spending the rest of the day rubbing the potatoes Nan had dug and laid on the black dirt to dry out didn't thrill me. It's the reason Anna Karenina hated inclement weather.

I slipped on my Russian rubber boots and trudged outside to where Nan was already rubbing. I squatted down beside her. "Nan, do you think I'm vain?"

Nan looked at me sideways. "What a question. Why would you ask such a thing?"

"I don't know."

"Who are you right now?"

I pointed to my rubber boots.

"Uh, Anna Karenina?" Nan didn't like it when I was Anna Karenina, and often voiced her regret for ever reading me that book. If I was Anna Karenina, that made her Countess Vronsky. The Countess got on Nan's nerves.

"Well, as Anna, I would say yes, as vain as the day is long. Anna lived her life seeing nothing around her—neither the poverty nor the injustice in society. All she chased was entertainment and avoiding boredom. Vain and selfish. Easy decisions, hard life. Hard decisions, easy life." Nan dropped a potato into the gunny sack. Her tone changed. "But as Celia Canterberry, the last thing you are is vain. I can hardly get you to comb your hair or wear your clothes the right side out. And think about all the earthworms you've saved. There's not a vain bone in your body."

"What about a miser? Am I one of those?"

"A miser? Where do you come up with these things? No, you are not a miser. Didn't you give your parents all your birthday money?"

My should-have-beens! I'd almost forgotten about that. When they came to rob Nan's house and couldn't find her stash, I gave them mine. "Yes, I did that."

Nan handed me a potato, and I rubbed all the dirt off before setting it into the gunny sack. "What about lust? Do you think I have that?"

Nan made a sound like she was about to swallow her tongue. "What has got into your head?"

"Yeah, you're probably right. I don't even play the lute."

We rubbed potatoes without speaking, I as Anna Karenina and Nan as Countess Vronsky. Both dreamy-eyed, thinking of better days. As we rubbed, I could sense the peasants mocking us from behind the caragana bushes. Nasty bunch. We moved from hill to hill, filling the gunny sacks to the brim. The entire time, I pictured in my mind's eye that magnificent clock. I was shaking my head whenever I thought it might strike the hour, when a new thought came to me. Nan! Who was going to shake their head for her?

"Nan, are *you* vain?" I tried to keep the panic out of my voice.

Nan stiffened beside me. "Why?"

"Just wondering."

"It's an odd thing for a little girl to wonder."

"Maybe here, but not if you're from Prague. Kids from Prague are obsessed with stuff like that. It keeps them up at night." I looked deep into her eyes, and asked her again. "Are you vain?"

"Oh, my God," Nan groaned, and threw a potato in the air. "You've been spending too much time with Dorigen."

12

Our neighbour, Mr. Douglas, with his cat Tiberius at his heels, came to lug the gunny sacks down into the cellar without Nan even asking. They came over after supper, Tiberius figure-eighting around his legs when he stopped at the garden's edge to survey the pile of gunny sacks.

"I know it's a lot, Walter." Nan bit her lip. "But if you don't mind, I'd be grateful."

Mr. Douglas grunted his response as he heaved the first sack over his shoulder. His mangy cat shifted on his haunches, waiting to pounce on any feeble-minded mouse foolish enough to have hidden under those potato sacks. Nan opened the screen door and ushered Mr. Douglas into her porch.

Nan's cellar wasn't the outside type, the kind fancy houses have, with big doors that fling open so a person can walk straight down into the basement in case of a tornado. No, her cellar was the covert kind. The kind that no one would know about unless a turncoat divulged the secret. Nan cleared the shoes that littered the floor in the porch closet and pulled the ring fastened to the trapdoor. My heart almost skipped a beat.

Although it seemed I'd always known of the cellar's

whereabouts, that dark gaping hole in the closet floor made me step back. Its blackness pulled at me. The hole was a four-foot drop to a dirt floor. And if a person survived the drop, they had to grope around for the pull string light. In the centre of the cellar there was another drop, and that's where Nan kept her store. Cabbages, turnips, beets, carrots and potatoes. In winter, when Nan was too tired or her back was acting up, she'd make me take the plunge. I'd sniff as I pulled on my Russian rubber boots. Once again, I was Anna Karenina. Doomed to a life of darkness. With a bucket in one hand, I'd root with the other in the various sacks, looking for whatever Countess Vronsky fancied for the evening meal. My misery was unending.

Before I started my rummaging, I'd carefully kick all the sacks, just to be on the safe side. One never knew what could be lurking about. And since St. Drogo—the only Catholic Church in Happy Valley—didn't have a manse, I figured Nan might stash the priest down there with a tin of Taster's Choice whenever the weather was uncooperative. It seemed only fitting since St. Drogo is the patron saint of unattractive people and coffee houses. Even Nan, who Old Lady Griggs said was no friend of papists, couldn't have a holy man roaming around back alleys like a lost pup trying to find some warm place to curl up in. The thought gave me a real sense of community.

But as winter waned and spring waxed, the firm fall harvest became soft and fuzzy at the edges, causing me to gag whenever I had to retrieve the decomposing corpses of Nan's crop: a black potato, a spongy carrot, an onion gone slick through the papery peel. Even Captain Ahab wouldn't have anything to do with the dirty business.

Now Mr. Douglas trudged into the porch and looked from the pit to Nan. His face was blotchy and his eyes wide. He was frozen to the spot, as if Nan had asked him to walk the plank. A soft look crossed Nan's face as she climbed down the hole instead.

Mr. Douglas, a little shaky, handed her the heavy sack. They repeated this until all the sacks were stored. Then Mr. Douglas leaned down to offer Nan a hand and hoist her out of the cellar opening. She brushed herself off and squeezed Mr. Douglas' arm. His eyes teared. Nan held her hand there, and he didn't move. They just looked at each other.

"A crack in the teacup," Mr. Douglas whispered.

"I know," Nan said softly.

My heart thumped against my ribs. I'd never heard Mr. Douglas say that before, but I don't think I was meant to. It was their own secret code, looking at each other and knowing things, just like Mr. Darcy and Elizabeth Bennet. Except Elizabeth was young and beautiful, and Mr. Darcy was rich and spoke in complete sentences.

Watching the two of them almost made me forget poor Anna Karenina. She'd be stuck down in that cellar unless there were vegetables to fetch or it was time for the spring planting. Poor thing, left to hide in amongst the burlap sacks, counting spiders to pass the time. If only she had a bit of lace to rub against her cheek, reminding her of better times and daylight. "Till we meet again," I whispered, as I rearranged the shoes over the trapdoor. I heard muffled weeping, and then the screen door creaked open.

I looked up to see Griggs come barging in. "Fresh off the presses," she called, waving the Happy Valley Journal above her head. Nan dropped her hand from Mr. Douglas' arm and turned towards the kitchen. "Anyone want a cup of coffee?" Before the words were out of her mouth, Mr. Douglas was gone.

Griggs took her spot at the kitchen table. "Do you need to ask?"

"Where's Walter?" Nan turned around, holding her Corningware percolator.

"How am I supposed to know?" Griggs spread the newspaper on the chrome table.

"You walked right past him."

Griggs sighed and looked up from the paper. "If I'd walked right past him, I'd be the first to say, wouldn't I?"

Nan made a little grunting sound at the back of her throat.

"Where's Celia?" Griggs asked.

I tapped her on the shoulder.

"Silly me, couldn't see for looking." Her lazy eye widened. "Look at this week's strip."

I nodded my head appreciatively. Griggs had done her usual embellishments, like giving Mrs. Whitford piggy trotters and making her beehive hair into a tornado with bulging-eyed baby animals holding on to the sticky hair-sprayed strands for dear life. "Love your choice of colours."

Griggs tilted her head back and forth. "I struggled with this one. We're having summer weather, but there is a bit of a nip in the air. And don't get me started on the light."

It was just like it used to be when Griggs and I would sit on her plastic-covered chesterfield, like compatriots in some Soviet spy movie. While Griggs and me went over the artistic merits of the comic strip, Nan must have been fuming beside us. She didn't seem to appreciate Griggs' artistic accomplishments. The only thing she noticed was the strip itself.

"When were you downtown, Celia Canterberry?"

I ran my eyes over the strip and there I was, sure as shootin. I was the only one with a seasonal head. In this strip I looked like a Dick and Jane reader, but everyone would know it was me. My hair was a dead giveaway. "This must have been drawn on my first day of school. That's the only time I got that close to Mrs. Whitford."

"I told you to stay away from that woman." Nan was almost

coming out of her skin.

"I would have, but you arranged for me to accompany Archibald, and I didn't want to walk the penitentiary fence on my own. And Farmer Hempel told me not to take the shortcut through his pasture. He said the wild roan cow would stomp me into the dirt. But besides all that…" I raised my eyebrows expectantly and waited for Nan to fill in the blank.

"Witches?" Nan pursed her lips and crossed her arms.

"Exactly. It wasn't my fault Mrs. Whitford was sticking her nose where it didn't belong." I pointed to the strip. "See? She's busybodying herself by spying on Oswald Elliot and Miss Dobbs."

Griggs' head snapped. "That's Oswald Elliot? I was so busy embellishing that it didn't dawn on me."

"He and Miss Dobbs were going at it like a cat and dog."

"Do you know why? I was so busy with the embellishment, I neglected to read the commentary."

"Something to do with her car tires." I could feel my face heat up.

Griggs clicked her tongue. "The way he's drawn, he looks like a young Robert Redford. If I'd known, I'd have given him a dose of reality."

"It's hard to do a self-portrait," I said. Griggs agreed. She said the only thing she got right with her own self-portrait was her pencil crayon hair colour.

"Do you know who's on the ladder? Not Amos Whitford, but the hunchback beside him."

"That's *Dr.* Whitford."

Griggs clicked her tongue. "Time hasn't been kind to him."

"I don't think that was time." I bent over the strip. "That was Oswald Elliot. Dr. Whitford is no Quasimodo, if you catch my drift. In the middle of their shouting match, Miss Dobbs turned and batted her eyelashes at the doctor."

"Well, isn't that a fine kettle of fish?"

"Celia," Nan interrupted. Her voice was as impatient as I'd ever heard it.

Griggs and me looked up from the comic. Nan was new to the game and didn't have the merits of comic strip perusing down pat like me and Griggs did. Griggs seemed irritated by the interruption. "Molly." She said in the same voice she used when I told her that being flummoxed wasn't the same as being constipated. "If you have something to add, wait your turn."

"My turn?"

"You heard me."

Nan set her Corningware percolator down in the middle of Griggs' freshly colored comic strip. "In my house, I don't have to wait my turn. All the turns are mine."

Griggs cleared her throat. "Your house?"

"Mmm hmm."

Griggs climbed on her rickety high horse. "If my memory serves me, this house," she waved her hand through the air, "the whole kit and caboodle, belongs to me." She looked Nan up and down. "Even that unfortunate ensemble."

Nan looked down at what she was wearing. "These are my gardening clothes."

"Mmm hmm. Say what you will, but *I* wouldn't greet company like that. And since this is one of my multiple properties...."

"Two. You have two. You can't count any better than you can spell your own name."

"So you admit it's my house." Griggs looked pleased with herself.

"I admit nothing."

"Oh, I heard you. You can't take it back now."

"We'll see about that." Nan grabbed her purse and coat and stormed out the door, leaving me alone with Griggs.

"Where do you think she's going?" I asked.

"To complain to the God-appointed mayor, no doubt. She's been threatening to do it every day since the auction."

"Will it make a difference?"

"Not likely."

I blew out my cheeks. "Do you think she realizes she has potato dirt on her face?"

"I doubt it. Not with her fashion sense." She waggled her eyebrows. "Now where were we?"

I pointed to the strip, and Griggs started reading. She used her Agnes Obermeyer voice.

Miss Dobbs, exhausted by her first day of grade two purgatory, aimlessly drives down Main Street not knowing what she is searching for. Then, she spots him when she least expects it. Her old love, her new whipping boy. This unnamed troubadour, unaware of her ire, strolls unguarded, searching for a muse, something to capture his interest. He hears his name called; he turns his head to parse the sound with a familiar lilt. His heart leaps. "My love," he coos.

But his affectionate tones are lost on Happy Valley's most venerable school teacher. As she slams her car door, she forgets her role as community leader and unleashes months of pent-up tension.

I tapped Griggs on the shoulder. "Miss Dobbs has been tense ever since she stopped meeting Oswald Elliot in the curling rink parking lot."

"Who told you that?"

"No one," I lied. It was Archibald, but Griggs didn't need to know that. And she didn't need to know that the morning after Archibald saw Oswald Elliot's bike peeking out of Miss Dobbs' car trunk was the happiest we'd ever seen that sour schoolmarm. Griggs' ambitious eye looked at me with more suspicion than her lazy one. To distract her, I pointed back at the strip.

Stepping into the broad chest of her past, the past she's tried to shake herself free of, her doe eyes fill with tears. "What are you trying to do to me?" Her delicate voice comes out barely more than a whisper.

"Do?" He runs a hand through his unmanaged locks, knowing the very act makes her tremble inside.

"Yes, do." Her eyes plead. "Seeing you at the window, nibbling on the sunflower seeds I'd left for the blue jays, it's more than I can handle."

"I was peckish."

Miss Dobbs nods. "I thought as much. Still, how do you expect me to teach when you know you're my biggest distraction?"

Sounding very much like Popeye, the amoureux lifts his chin, places his hands on his hips and looks into the middle distance. "I am what I am." He knows that he is her Popeye, and she is his Olive Oyl.

He sighs. His Olive Oyl's gaze has flitted towards the daft and gluttonous face of Brutus, the hunchbacked brute who stands on a ladder just to claim he's the bigger man.

My eyes scanned every panel of the strip. I didn't even have a speaking part. "What about me? This is supposed to be my comic strip. I'm supposed to be the star."

"I know," Griggs said, patting the back of my hand. "But you stuck your tongue out at Mrs. Whitford. Something thousands would tremble at."

"Where?"

Griggs pointed, and I leaned closer, examining my Dick and Jane reader head. "I thought that was a bookmark."

Griggs looked at me like I was a peasant. "Perhaps to the untrained eye."

Griggs and me were still discussing my comic book adventures when Nan came storming back into the kitchen. I didn't know how long she'd been gone. All I knew was that she was madder than when she left.

"What did the mayor say?" Griggs asked, as sweet as can be.

"He said that the house is yours and there is not a thing I can do about it."

"That's what I thought." Griggs stood and stretched. "I should get going. Mr. Griggs will wonder where I got off to." She patted me on the top of the head. "And the next time I see you, we'll talk about the colour of this kitchen."

———

That night when Nan was tucking me in, I reached out and took hold of her arm the way she'd held Mr. Douglas' over the cellar door. It didn't feel dreamy and Nan's cheeks didn't flush, but she paused and looked down at me. "A crack in the teacup," I said.

"You heard that, did you?"

I nodded. "What does it mean?"

Nan asked me to scooch over. She folded her hands in her lap and let out a long breath. "It's from a poem Walter used to read to me. By W. H. Auden, I think. Not all of it comes to mind, but one verse steals its way into my recollection. Steals and sticks there. *And the crack in the teacup opens a lane to the land of the dead.*"

"What's it mean?"

"I'm not sure I know myself. Perhaps," she turned away and went quiet. "Perhaps, it's all about snippets of time. And the things that can't be taken back. As they say, once a bell is rung."

"Forget the bell. Is Mr. Douglas the teacup?"

"I suppose."

"And he's cracked because of the war?"

"Maybe."

"And that's why he can't be my could-have-been grandpa?"

Nan patted my arm before leaving me to finish my prayers on my own.

13

Saturday morning had barely opened its eyes when Nan popped out of bed. She was more eager to get to the library than usual. "Hurry up, Celia," she said, tapping her foot as she waited on the corner. "I'm not getting any younger."

When I caught up to her, she frowned and looked me up and down. "Why are you walking like that?"

I wasn't walking anymore peculiar than I usually did. I hadn't let loose my draggy leg, or adjusted my bolty neck. But in my hurry to leave the house, I had put my pinchy church shoes on the wrong feet. And the tacks I'd pushed through their worn treads—to mimic a Lawrence Welk tap dancer—were poking into my freshly scrubbed soles. I scowled. How those women could smile through the agony was beyond me.

"Why do we always have to dress up to go to the library?"

"Celia, if I've told you once, I've told you a hundred times. Church is a place of prayer, libraries are a place of higher learning. We treat each with equal reverence."

Nan was right, I'd heard it before, but I liked making her say it anyway. "What about school? Isn't that a place of higher learning?"

"School is an unavoidable necessity."

"I think last time you called it the halls of disillusionment."

"Now you're splitting hairs." She pulled open a large oak door. "After you, milady."

I limped past, walking as softly as I could. Nan thought I was being respectful, but she didn't know about the tacks. When she'd noticed they were missing from the corkboard in the kitchen, I told her that Tiberius must have eaten them when Mr. Douglas was putting the potatoes in the cellar. Nan sighed and pinned the church bulletin to the corkboard with her favourite brooch.

"What kind of book are you going to get this time?" I asked.

"Well, I'm not sure. I'll have to look at them first. Whichever one speaks to me."

All the books spoke to me. Some screamed *stay away*; others whispered, *over here, Celia, over here.*

By the time we reached the front desk, Miss Libby, the librarian, broke into a smile and waved us over. "Oh, it's so nice to see you, Molly." She winked. "I've put the book you asked for aside. But I don't know why you were so secretive about it."

"I have my reasons." Nan turned the book over in her hand.

I stood on my toes, better to see the cover. *Squatters, Pirates and Protesters*. "What are squatters?"

"Something that will take the wind out of Dorigen's sails." She patted me on the head. We had turned to wander down the marvelous aisles, when Miss Libby called us back.

"Before I forget," she said, leaning farther across the counter. "We just got some new books in that I think you'll love."

"Are there any suitable for Celia?" Nan asked.

"Well, I don't know. You and I are very different in that area.

You've read her books I wouldn't let her touch until she's an adult. But far be it from me to tell you how to raise your granddaughter."

Miss Libby was on slippery ground. God help her if she mentioned Audrey, my should-have-been ma. If she did, Nan would hit the roof. And it might be the last time we stepped foot in the local library. She lowered her voice and leaned closer to Nan so I wouldn't hear. I inclined my head.

"One of the books I'm talking about we keep behind the counter. A little too steamy for the average reader, with all the," she lowered her voice again, "S. E. X."

"What's sex?" I waggled my eyebrows at Nan.

Nan dropped her gaze to me and groaned. "It's an entire book about dangling participles."

"Oh. I wouldn't like that."

"No, you wouldn't."

Miss Libby rummaged around behind the desk and held up a novel. "*From Here to Eternity.*" It was her turn to waggle her eyebrows.

"That was published years ago," Nan said, opening the cover.

"It took that long for the library board to allow it on the premises. Wheels turn slowly in Happy Valley."

While they talked, I slipped away unnoticed, but I didn't go to the kids' section like I usually did. This time I weaved my way up and down the long lines of shelves. Looking, looking, until lo-and-behold, there they were, all twenty volumes of the World Book Encyclopedia. If Nan would read them to me, Archibald would never be able to outsmart me. I took the A book off the shelf; if Nan worked hard at it, we could be through this by Christmas. I lugged it back to Nan.

"For land sakes, what do you want to do with that?" Nan looked aghast at the tome.

"I want you to read it to me instead of our regular books."

Miss Libby furrowed her brow. "I think you'd enjoy *From Here to Eternity* more."

Nan ignored Miss Libby. "You'd rather have this than all our wonderful adventures?"

I nodded.

She flipped open to the first page and started reading. *"A is the first letter of our alphabet. It was the first letter in all the alphabets from which ours evolved. The Semites, who lived in Syria and Palestine, named their first letter aleph, meaning ox."*

I held up my hand. If that's what it took to be Archibald-smart, I'd rather be Celia-dumb. "Can you skip ahead? There's got to be better stuff."

Nan flipped a clump of pages and read on. *"Astronomy is the study of the stars, planets, and other objects that make up the universe. Astronomers observe the locations and motions of heavenly bodies. However, almost all astronomers are interested in more than just observing these objects."*

"That's boring," I interrupted, disappointed not only with Nan's lack of oratorical flourish, but also with Archibald. When she recited her spiel on the Prague clock, I thought she was so nervous she left out the most interesting bits—like the part where the clockmaker's brother fell out of the bell tower when he was caught wearing ladies' pantyhose—but Archibald never mentioned a word about that. Sure, I made that part up, but it could have had a sliver of truth. Odds were the clockmaker had a brother that died, right?

Irritation got the best of me. "Where are the swords? Where are the dragons?"

"The swords would be under S, and the dragons would be under D."

"Do they fight anybody?"

"No. Dragons would be classified as mythical creatures. And

the entry for swords will contain information about how they were forged and the emblems on their hilts."

"Who cares about that kind of stuff?"

"The people who wrote this book."

"I'm putting it back."

"Wise choice."

Lugging that book the second time was much more of a chore. Boring things carried more weight. The spot I'd pulled the World Book from was too tight to be comfortable, so I searched the shelf for a roomier space and slid the disappointment in. Archibald could have her encyclopaedias; I'd stick with Captain Ahab. Just then I heard the clinking of glass, as if Ahab were toasting to my safe return to the ship. I followed the clinks and muffled chit chat until I came to a back room—room for special meetings and shotgun weddings.

I opened the door a crack and peered inside. At the head of a large table sat Billy Billboson, his bombastic melon perched precariously on his stickman neck. Larry, Moe, and Curly, the only hairs on his head, lay passively as if they'd given up on life. Leonard Hoopenmire and his two brothers sat next to Billy. Leonard looked bored to tears; lucky for him, his mother kept jamming a finger between his shoulder blades to keep him lively. Next was Bartholomew Dankworth, making fart noises with his armpit. His widowed mother didn't stop him, because everyone in Happy Valley knew the Dankworths didn't have a piano. They were a *make the best with what you have* kind of family. Farther down the table, Sally Shephard bit at her mustache, while Eugenia Whitford sat bookended by her two Whitford cousins. Eugenia was doing her best to look sweet and empty-headed. All in all, it was a motley crew, but I knew exactly what these ne'er-do-wells were up to.

It was the monthly meeting of the European Cheese Tasters. Mrs. Whitford was fond of saying that being a Cheese Taster should be a prerequisite to joining the Ladies of the Perpetual Indigence Society. And even though most of the Cheese Tasters were boys, all bow-tied and brylcreemed, that didn't bother the PIS ladies. Since most of them were incapable of having daughters, candy-assed boys were all they could hope for.

And there amid everything was the pissiest one of them all, Mrs. Whitford, my number one nemesis. My lip curled at the sight of her. Flanking her on one side was Miss Dobbs, and on the other, Mrs. Figgler. My number two and three nemesisuess. I felt like Macbeth stumbling upon Flo, Vi, and Ru, stirring their cauldron and arguing about who forgot the eye of newt. But on closer examination, they could have been the living embodiment of Archibald's clock. Mrs. Whitford, always bragging about her drugstore and fancy car, was the epitome of greed. Miss Dobbs, worrying if she smelled like pee or had a run in her stocking, was vanity incarnate. And Mrs. Figgler in her muumuu—well, what better example of worldly pleasure could I image than a woman who had abandoned waistbands entirely to peddle fresh-baked cookies and lemonade? The only thing missing was Old Lady Griggs ringing a bell.

But what were Miss Dobbs and Mrs. Figgler doing here? They didn't have children. This group was for mothers who were proud of their offspring. At least, that's the reason Nan said we couldn't join—because Nan was more than a mother; she was my *grand*mother. I considered the two tetchy outsiders. Miss Dobbs was likely standing in for Eugenia's dead mother, since I knew she had ambitions towards Eugenia's father, just like with everyone else who read the Happy Valley Journal. But why was Mrs. Figgler there? She was angling to become a PIS lady, I bet, by ingratiating herself with Mrs. Whitford.

Mrs. Whitford cleared her throat and began reading from the Cheese Taster's manual: "Here we have a cheese from Bavaria. As you can see, it's semi-soft with a natural rind. The texture is a complex mixture of not too dense, not too soft, just right firmness. A cheese lover's delight with the smoky aroma of applewood."

"Oh, yuck," I groaned. The description was giving me a stomach ache.

Mrs. Whitford looked up in the utterance's direction. Her eyes locked on mine and she snapped the book shut. "What are you doing here?" Her two little girls, who looked as confused as baby owls flung from their nest, swung their empty heads in my direction. The smallest of the two grabbed hold of her miniscule pigtails and burst into tears.

"I'm not going to ask again," Mrs. Whitford yelled. "What are you doing here?"

"You just asked again. Sheesh. You're about as good at math as Mussolini." I casually leaned against the door frame and examined my fingernails. "But the real question is, what are any of us doing here? Old Lady Griggs says that's the mystery of the ages."

It was the wrong thing to say. Mrs. Whitford looked from Miss Dobbs to Mrs. Figgler, and then the three of them glared at me in unison, as if it had been choreographed. Miss Dobbs grabbed Eugenia and the owl children in a comforting smother while Mrs. Whitford and Mrs. Figgler threw themselves at me. It happened so fast I barely dodged the onslaught. (I could thank Miss Dobbs for my highly tuned dexterity.) Before Mrs. Whitford and Mrs. Figgler had a chance to regroup, I was sprinting back to Nan, my thumbtack tap shoes announcing my retreat.

Nan and Miss Libby were still talking about me when I skidded to a stop.

"As I was saying," Miss Libby said, putting Nan's new tomes into the book bag, "far be it from me to tell you how to raise your granddaughter."

"Let's keep it that way," Nan said, cutting off the librarian.

Miss Libby reddened as she handed Nan the bag.

"It was nice chatting," Nan said, as she stuck out her hand for me. Nan strolled out of the library as if she didn't have a care in the world. I limped out, all the while looking over my shoulder at Mrs. Whitford and Mrs. Figgler, who fumed between the magazine rack and foreign book display.

Nan turned and followed my gaze. "I think I know that woman," she said. "But for the life of me, I can't place her."

"It's Mrs. Whitford, your boss's wife."

"I know that," Nan snapped. "It's the other one, the one in the muumuu."

I shrugged. "She looks like a Flo to me."

14

"I'm accompanying you home," I said to Archibald at recess.

Archibald squeezed my hand. "Your Nan doesn't mind?"

"Nope. She's working more hours at the Happy Valley Druggist and would rather me walk with you than hang out with Griggs."

"I'm so glad."

"And we can sneak into your mom's library and stare at the clock."

Archibald nodded. The smile on her face said she couldn't think of anything finer to do. It almost made the prospect of USSR after recess bearable. But Miss Dobbs prevailed, and it was as boring as she intended it to be. She'd swept away the sunflower seeds from the outside window ledge, so there weren't even any blue jays to watch. And if Oswald Elliot was anywhere about, he was staying clear. Miss Dobbs had slid open all the classroom windows and taken off the screens so that if his head popped up she could whack him.

"Put a sweater on," she told us before we sat down. "There's a cool breeze. Don't want any of you to get the sniffles."

Each time Miss Dobbs passed the bank of windows, she cracked her open palm with a yardstick. It made me wonder if she was thinking about the comic strip. The one thing that seemed to bring her comfort was patting Eugenia's shoulder whenever she clip-clopped by.

Griggs had said that particular comic strip was Oswald Elliot's artistic tribute to Miss Dobbs. "Do you think she enjoys being compared to Olive Oyl?" I asked. Griggs had tilted her head back and forth. "That depends. Miss Dobbs isn't a natural beauty, but then again neither is her cartoon counterpart. Like Olive Oyl, she's coy and thin, and that's enough for some chaps to fall in love. But I daresay it's hard to know how to please a woman like that."

My gaze flitted from the bank of windows to my Dick and Jane reader as I replayed the conversation with Griggs in my head. Miss Dobbs was getting tied in knots. Each time she paced by the windows, she growled. Timmy Crybaby-Head would not make it to the end of the day. Those plaid pants weren't going to hide it. And sitting in cold pee would do nothing to improve his disposition.

I raised my hand. "He's not coming."

"Who?"

"Your comic strip amoureux."

Miss Dobbs' cheeks reddened. "He's not my amoureux." She swatted her palm before barreling towards me. "Who asked you anyway?"

"Nobody."

"Then keep your idiotic comments to yourself."

I kept my idiotic comments to myself for the rest of the day. Even when Miss Dobbs called on me to answer the simplest questions. "Celia?" I didn't look up from colouring my map of Canada. "What's the capital of Saskatchewan?"

I shrugged my shoulders.

"The capital of Canada?"

I shrugged again.

"Surely you know the capital of something? You wouldn't shut up about them yesterday."

That was yesterday. Yesterday I wasn't told to keep my idiotic comments to myself. Yesterday I hadn't tried to show her I understood her frustration. I was used to being drawn in all the wrong ways, making things seem different from what they were, and I could sympathize. Yesterday I made myself tolerate Miss Dobbs, but today I allowed myself to despise her. And I hoped, in my heart of hearts, that in her old age she'd be stuck alongside Mrs. Figgler in a cast-off muumuu, spending her days eating rock hard cookies, smelling each other's cheesy farts, and wondering where it had all gone wrong. The Abbott and Costello of Happy Valley.

"Do you want to stay after class?" Miss Dobbs asked, interrupting that delightful musing.

I pushed back my bangs and narrowed my eyes before mouthing the words, *Do you want to keep me*?

Miss Dobbs turned to Timmy Crybaby-Head, cracking his desktop with her yardstick. Poor Timmy didn't stand a chance.

15

When the bell rang, I was itching to escape. In a clipped tone, Miss Dobbs told us to have a good afternoon as she stared out the window. We all knew she didn't mean it. It was just something they taught her to say at Teachers' College. That, and wash your hands after anything involving bodily fluid.

Archibald and me checked out all the low spots on the path to her house, the places that collected water after a light rain. The recent warm weather had prevented any pooling, which was good for the earthworms, but disappointing for us. I kicked a pebble down the dirt path.

"Helen," I said, in my best British accent. "You look rather well."

Archibald stopped short and licked her lips. She was trying to figure out what storybook character I was playing. There were many, but only one with a friend named Helen.

"Jane Eyre," I whispered.

"Jane," Archibald squeezed my hand. "I've been meaning to tell you that the frock you're wearing today is particularly lovely."

I did a little curtsy. "I sewed it in the dark."

"I thought as much."

We wandered along the ribbon path, taking turns curtsying and hand squeezing, so preoccupied that we completely forgot Mrs. Figgler. She was waiting for us on her lopsided porch swing.

"There you are, girls!" Her voice was mean enough to match her house. "What took you so long?"

"We had school," Archibald called back, but I knew she instantly regretted it. We had promised to ignore Mrs. Figgler, no matter how much she pestered us.

"Your brothers have been home for at least half an hour," she scolded. "And then you two come lollygagging along as if I have nothing better to do with my time than wait."

Both Archibald and me didn't know what to say and neither of us wanted to ask why she was waiting because that would mean we cared. But Mrs. Figgler didn't notice our reluctance. She cleared her throat and stood, causing the lopsided swing to shake off its weariness and right itself. "I would like to introduce my son," she said with the wave of her hand.

We scanned her yard. There was no one there. I looked at Archibald and made the cuckoo sign. "Nice to meet you," I said to the air, as Archibald and me backed away slowly.

Mrs. Figgler rolled her eyes. "Skinny," she said. "Stand and show yourself."

A full-grown man popped from behind a scraggly rosebush. His hair was pulled back in a ponytail, and he wasn't wearing a shirt. Unlike Mayor Forde, his skin held him in tightly. Deep lines and creases sectioned off his torso. Old Lady Griggs would call him chiselled, but not too loud in case Mr. Griggs got a complex. His chiselled-ness caused Archibald and me to stare. He should have been the Cheese Tasters' mascot; that would show the citizens of Happy Valley what a candy-ass boy could turn into.

"That's not what Mr. Douglas looks like," I whispered to Archibald. "I saw him in his altogether the day he ambled over to Nan's house all lost and forlorn. He was full of hair bunches and age spots." I stood on my tiptoes to get a better look. "I can't see Skinny's dangling participle, so can't comment in that department. Can't even be sure he has one."

"I've wanted to introduce him to your mother," Mrs. Figgler said, trying to pull our gaze off her son. "But haven't seen hide nor hair of her all day."

Archibald and me both nodded as Skinny flexed his hide and hairs.

"Let her know, will you? She's not wearing her mourning colours anymore, so it wouldn't be considered unseemly." She paused and put a finger to the side of her nose. "And tell her that Skinny's not afraid of spiders. Not even black widows."

Archibald and me backed away from Mrs. Figgler and her rippled son, all the way to Archibald's doorstep. I whispered, "Is your mother looking for a new man?"

Archibald shook her head. "I don't think so. She says she's exhausted and doesn't want any more changes to our family."

My eyes were still on Skinny. He was standing poker straight, his hands on his hips, his faced turned into the light breeze. "He's kind of nice to look at."

Archibald nodded as we slipped into the house, down the hallway, and through those magnificent library doors. We panted a little under the clock, enjoying our quick escape. But as the skeleton rang the bell, in my mind's eye all I could see was Skinny, and I shuddered.

16

Instead of going straight home, I went to Old Lady Griggs' house. I didn't even stop by Farmer Hempel's cow pasture. Today wasn't the day I wanted Samwise Gamgee to ignore me. I needed answers, and I knew Griggs would have some of them. The rest she could make up. She and Mr. Griggs were having their afternoon tea when I stepped through the door.

Griggs paused mid-pour. "Am I watching you this afternoon?"

I shook my head.

"Is your Nan all right?"

"I think she's still at work."

Griggs sat down. "I've already collected the rent, so it's not that." She eyed me suspiciously. "You're not going to talk about dangling participles are you?"

"No. I wanted to ask you about Archibald's mom. Do you think she wants a new husband?"

"How am I supposed to know?"

I shrugged. "Woman's intuition, I guess."

Griggs lit up. "There's no guessing about it, that woman likes her men. I don't think there was a suitor she turned away.

She might as well have marched down the aisle blindfolded. Probably was when she married Earl McGinty. That was a no-account man if ever there was one. And ugly as a spider. Still, she claimed she was meant to bring untold happiness to those whose lives were destined to be short."

Griggs ambled into the living room and came back with the big black scrapbook. "I've been waiting for you to ask. There's so much to talk about. Your Nan made me promise not to open that Pandora's Box unless you brought it up first. And let me tell you, it's been a month of Sundays." She retook her seat. "The part that interests folks most is their demise." Griggs' lazy eye was pinpoint serious as she flipped the pages. "Oswald Elliot made a poem out of the whole sordid affair. That way when another husband dies, he only has to add a verse, and the townsfolk have no doubt about what really happened. Mayor Forde thinks it's Oswald's civic duty to help prevent gossip and educate all at the same time. Wouldn't want anyone thinking she's killing her husbands almost as fast as she can marry them. It's God that strikes them down. Don't ask me why. Some things are meant to stay mysterious—like toe fungus and botulism. Mr. Griggs suffered from one and died of the other. Poor dear. Never wanted to go barefoot in public." She reached over and patted his stuffed hand.

"Thank God Oswald's poem sets folks straight. Not about botulism or toe fungus—he doesn't have the chops to write a poem like that. No, his poem concentrates on death. Just like the poem that helps us remember King Henry the Eighth's wives: Divorced, beheaded, died / Divorced, beheaded, survived. Except Oswald's poem is more Shakespearian."

Griggs was right; in the strip, each of Mrs. Willoughby's husbands were featured in their own frame with a line of verse to spell out their end. In the first square was Grenway Tibbs. He was hit by the train while walking across a trestle. Bose Malloy was next, he got lost and froze to death in a snow storm. Then there was Archibald Quigley. He was struck by lightning. Buttons Malloy got rabies. Earl McGinty got stung to death by bees, and Sly Willoughby drowned when his car was washed off the road during that terrible storm last summer. Griggs called it an avalanche of death. She cleared her throat and began to read.

> *Grenway Tibbs was crossing the tracks, was hit by a train. Now he's not coming back.*
>
> *Bose Malloy, as strong as an ox, got stuck in a snowdrift and came home in a box.*
>
> *Archibald Quigley, so sprite and so spry, rode his bike through a meadow. How fast he did fry.*
>
> *Buttons Malloy, brother to Bose, was bit by a dog and went mad to his toes.*
>
> *Earl McGinty, so brave and so true, stepped on a hive, and now he's quite blue.*
>
> *Sly Willoughby, the best of the bunch, used his car for a boat, don't expect him for lunch."*

Griggs went on, telling me a lot more than I wanted to know. She called Archibald and her siblings the graveside babies. I didn't like that. It made them sound grimy with open sores. And she told me what I already knew, that Mrs. Willoughby named each of her children after their fathers, as a living tribute. When I asked her if she liked any of Mrs. Willoughby's husbands, Griggs said they weren't around long enough to like or dislike, except for Earl McGinty. He had been around far too long, as far as she was concerned. Apparently, Earl called Griggs 'the buggy-eyed shrew with a hobo for a husband.'

I tried to listen over my grumbling belly, since Griggs didn't offer me a drink or one of her overcooked biscuits, but I was fading away. When Griggs finished talking about Archibald's dads, she changed the topic to Mr. Griggs' gout.

"I got to get going," I said. "Nan's probably home, and I want to ask her about Archibald's new neighbour."

Griggs' head snapped to attention. "Archibald has a new neighbour? How did I not know that?"

I shrugged. "She's new."

"You said that."

"And she has a son who's not afraid of spiders, not even black widows. We saw him without his shirt on."

"Not afraid of black widows? How would you know that?

"Mrs. Figgler told us."

"She did, did she?"

I nodded again.

Griggs grunted. "The impertinence of that woman. An outsider making a veiled reference like that. She's got the nerve. If she were a taxpaying Happy Valleyan that would be one thing, but a virtual stranger? And as if Archibald's mother would knock off all those husbands. One could happen to anyone, two if she got a taste for it, but six? That's just plain wasteful." Griggs contemplated for a while before flipping to a different page in the scrapbook. "Archibald's mother has a type. For second-graders like you, that means the kind of man she tends to be attracted to." Her bony finger jabbed the paper. "Does the Figgler fellow look like this?"

I shook my head. "Mrs. Figgler's son has longer hair and no shirt."

"Lucky for us, Oswald Elliot draws everyone with their clothes on, so concentrate on the face."

Griggs flipped pages for me to examine faces, like a police lineup. But even after going through all six husbands, I couldn't tell if the men were similar and belonged to a type.

"Mrs. Figgler's son is all ripples."

"What do you mean, all ripples? You're too young to notice such things."

"Mrs. Figgler is hoping Archibald's mom will notice."

"How do you know?"

"She told us. His name is Skinny."

"Skinny Figgler? What a ridiculous name." She reached over and patted her husband's hand. "Mr. Griggs is horrified. I can tell by the way he stiffens."

I looked at Mr. Griggs. He was as floppy as usual, his cotton-stuffed head lolling to one side.

"And," Griggs fumed, a finger stabbing the air, "as for this interloper trotting her son out like some prize stallion, we'll see about that. Thinks he can prance into this town and snap up the newest widow? And a moneyed widow at that? Lacey Willoughby needs me whether she likes it or not."

I learned a few things from Griggs that afternoon, not the least of which was that Griggs didn't like the name Skinny and that Archibald's mother's Christian name was Lacey. It was the first time I'd heard it. Lacey. It suited her.

But best of all, I found out that Griggs was forming a plan to thwart Skinny Figgler and his menacing mother. But my stomach rumbling prevented me from investigating further. If I didn't hightail it out of there, I'd faint with hunger.

17

The next day Griggs was standing outside the school when Archibald and me came strolling out. We stopped short. "What are you doing here?" I asked.

Griggs sniffed as she adjusted her honeymoon hat. "No hello? How are you?"

"Hello. How are you?" I parroted. "What are you doing here?"

"I've come to accompany you."

"Where?"

"To Archibald's, silly." She held out her shepherd's pie.

"We don't want that," Archibald whispered.

I nodded, but wasn't sure how to tell Griggs. She had her heart set on giving up that pie, and once Griggs got her heart set on something, neither hell nor high water would stop her. Griggs' shepherd's pie was infamous. She'd been schlepping the same pie to funerals and birthdays since before I was born. And in turn, each of the recipients would schlepp it back, making it the best aged pie in the county. Mayor Forde had once mistaken it for something edible. It gave him the trots for nearly a week.

"What did she say?" Griggs snapped. "I don't sanction whispering."

"Neither do I," I said, swatting Archibald's arm.

She swatted me back. "*I'll never play on your sailboat bed again*," she mouthed.

My throat went dry. That was the worst threat Archibald could make. The thought of telling Captain Ahab almost broke my heart.

I looked directly into Griggs' ambitious eye. "Although we appreciate the offer..."

Archibald nodded.

"We're on a diet," I said.

"This isn't for you!" Griggs looked appalled. "It would be wasted on a child's palette. I've come to accompany you, you ninnies."

"But I'm the accompanier," I said.

"To hell with that," Griggs said, tightening her grip on the pie. "Two little girls walking all on their own, coming across God knows what? Does that sound safe to you?"

I shrugged, chiding myself. I'd looked in the wrong eye.

Griggs took off, steaming towards Archibald's house. She didn't even check to see if we were following.

"It's probably safer this way," I said. "Griggs is the poster ogre for why children shouldn't walk alone." I could feel the relief leaving Archibald's rigid body.

"Do we have to keep up, Jane?"

"Nope. She won't even notice. But thank you for asking, Helen." I curtsied.

Helen linked my arm, and we perused the ground for languishing earthworms, the pale, bloated little devils who were no longer treading water.

"Look, Jane."

I followed Helen's gaze. A troupe of ants were shouldering a dried-up earthworm. "State funeral," I said. "Must have been a dignitary."

Helen and I placed our hands over our hearts and sang *God Save the Queen*. We were moved beyond tears and had to blow our noses on our sleeves. After all was said and done, Archibald wanted to know what God was saving the queen from.

"A bad marriage," I replied. "They behead queens willy-nilly over there. And then, of course, there's the witches."

Archibald gasped.

"And those poor evil dears, they burn at the stake. No matter how you slice it, England's not a safe place for women."

Archibald started a whole new verse of *Jesus Loves Me*, one I'd never heard before. By the time we reached her house, her voice was hoarse, and Griggs was coming undone.

"Where have you two been?" she said, peeking out from behind a young elm tree. The thin sapling gave her little cover.

"We had to stop for a funeral procession."

Griggs' eyebrows furrowed. "What kind of idiot would have a funeral procession along a dirt path?"

"It wasn't an idiot; it was a dignitary."

Griggs dismissed me with a wave, her attention turning back to the Figglers. Her beady eyes scanned their yard. "Is that the scoundrel you were talking about? The fool that can't afford clothes?" She pointed at Skinny Figgler, who ran his fingers through his long blond mane before picking up a pair of shears.

"Yup. But he's wearing pants."

"Kind of has to if he's pruning. One slip and he's a girl. Still, I don't think he's much to look at. Shiny with perspiration, yes, and rippled, as you called it. But the way he tosses those locks, he's going to put his back out."

Archibald and me tucked up beside her. "Then why are you staring?"

"Just being neighbourly." Griggs' gaze didn't seem neighbourly. It seemed like something that might land her in the Happy Valley Penitentiary. "And you're sure his name is Skinny?"

"That's what Mrs. Figgler said."

"Never met a Skinny before. So, as you can imagine, I don't have a point of reference." Griggs sucked her cheeks. "Usually when I hear a name, I compare it to all the others I know by the same name. Hate one person by a certain name, hate them all. A leopard never changes his spots. And a name never changes its letters."

"Makes sense," I said.

"Saves me all kinds of time. Say, do you know anyone named Dennis?"

"No, I don't think so."

Griggs fixed me with her wandering eye. "Keep it that way."

Skinny paused to wipe his brow and arch his back in the sun. Griggs almost licked her lips. She didn't drop her gaze, even when Mrs. Figgler told her to move along, that her son wasn't putting on a public service for the sake of a shrivelled old woman. Griggs snorted and stayed where she was.

"Did you hear me?" Mrs. Figgler snapped. "I can see you leering from behind that tree."

"I'm not leering, I'm contemplating," Griggs snapped back. "Not sure if I want to give you my shepherd's pie."

"I don't want it." Mrs. Figgler grabbed a broom and hefted it over her head as if she were some circus strongman. Her muumuu did a Marilyn Monroe billow, revealing meaty, unshaven legs.

Archibald and me had never seen anything like it. It was like looking into the future at an older version of Miss Dobbs, one with a sharper tongue and rounder edges, who'd given up all hope. Old Lady Griggs' eyes steadied and her fingers dug into her dish.

"I've gotten rid of vermin before," Mrs. Figgler warned, and broke the broom handle over her knee.

I pulled on Griggs. "It's time to go. You're accompanying us, remember?"

Griggs shook me off. "It's time to go when I say it's time to go."

"But Mr. Griggs will be worried."

"He'll be fine. He's a grown man."

"Listen to the child." Mrs. Figgler moved closer with a piece of broom handle in each hand. "Now I told you to move off."

"It's a free country." Griggs ducked as Mrs. Figgler launched part of the handle in her direction. It twisted and turned like an Olympic javelin, catching the side of Griggs' pie and dashing it to the ground. Caught up in the excitement, Skinny stepped behind his mother, flexed, and bared his teeth.

"Actually, it's a Constitutional Monarchy with a Parliamentary Democracy," I said, and Archibald snickered like a horse.

Griggs and Figgler turned on me in unison. "Oh, shut up, you little know-it-all."

The words seemed to trigger something in Griggs. Forgetting all about her infamous dish, her lazy eye focused and she stepped out from behind the tree. "I know you," she said to Mrs. Figgler, confusion in her voice. "Either that, or this is déjà vu."

"It's not déjà anything. You don't know me, so get the hell off my property!"

Griggs squinted her one good eye. "I never forget a face, especially when it belongs to someone I don't like."

"Well, you can't forget a face you've never seen." Mrs. Figgler hurled what was left of her broom at Griggs and howled like a madwoman.

Archibald ran screaming into her house.

Skinny whimpered from a pulled muscle.

Mrs. Figgler said it was his own damn fault for posing like a strongman and boxed him in the ear. She said he was supposed to strut for Archibald's mom, not some dried-up prune Hades had rejected.

All the while, Old Lady Griggs just stood there as if her feet were nailed to the spot. I had to slap her pretty hard on the bottom to get her moving. But eventually, we headed home.

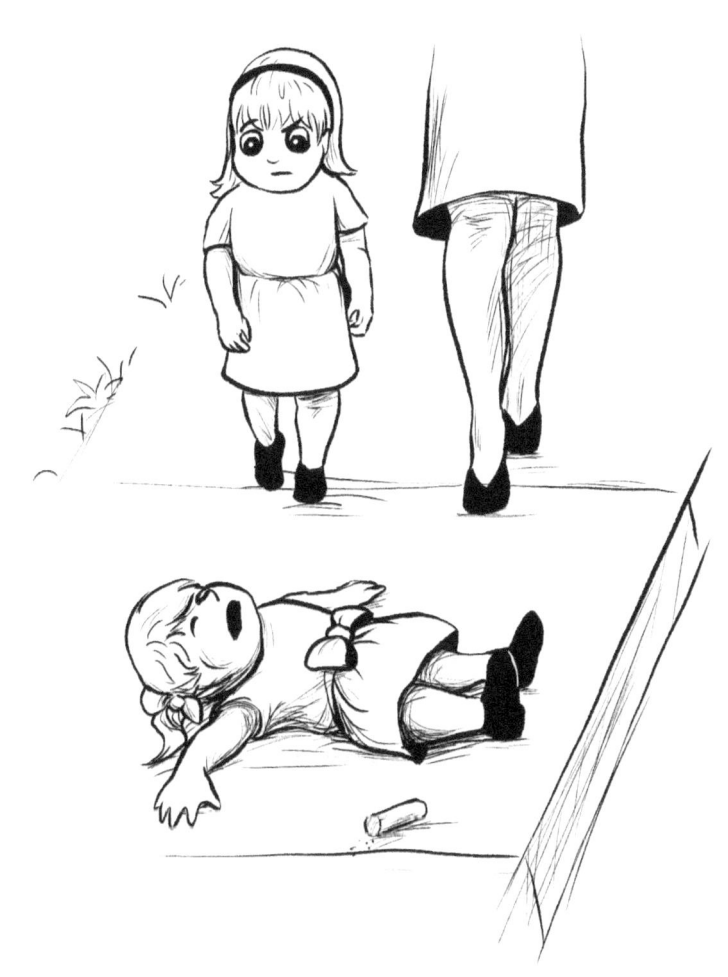

18

Griggs mumbled all the way back to her house. She didn't even notice when one of Mrs. Whitford's owl children lay prone on the sidewalk, waiting for a passerby to draw her outline with pink chalk, like a dead person. Griggs almost stepped on one of her little owl fingers. The child squawked, causing Mrs. Whitford to storm out of the Happy Valley Druggist with maternal concern. I tucked myself in close to the shadows to avoid being mistaken for the culprit. But as soon as Mrs. Whitford's gaze latched onto Griggs' backside, she knew who to blame.

"Why they let cows in honeymoon hats stroll down Main Street, I'll never know."

Griggs didn't turn on her heel or make an obscene gesture, like I expected. She was too busy muttering *"I know that woman,"* over and over again. I was disappointed in her; Griggs missed a plum opportunity to guess this week's shade of Mrs. Whitford's trotter nail polish. We left her raging on the sidewalk.

The only thing left to do was play twenty questions. "Is Mrs. Figgler a relative?" I asked, loping beside Griggs to keep up.

"I don't think so," Griggs said, furrowing her brow. "But Mr. Griggs' family has a few odd ducks, if you know what I mean."

"Did you go to school with her?"

"Not sure."

"A childhood neighbour?"

"Could be."

We went on like this all the way to Griggs' house. When we parted at the end of her drive, she turned and patted me on the head. "Thanks for helping me narrow it down, Celia."

"No problem," I said, and skipped off.

I called for Captain Ahab as soon as I stepped foot in Nan's house. He was up on my sailboat bed, rigging the mast. All day long he had sat in the back of my mind, biding his time, waiting for Queequeg to join him. I took the stairs two at a time and was away sailing the Pequod before I could get my shoes off. We had sailed around the world twice when I heard Nan come through the screen door.

"Celia," she called.

I looked at Captain Ahab. He shook his head.

"Celia," she called again.

Once more the captain shook his head.

"So help me," I heard Nan say. "QUEEQUEG!" This time Nan's tone was verging on unacceptable.

"Aye, aye, matey," I called back.

The sound of Nan's hard-soled shoes came up the stairs. She hesitated outside my bedroom door. "Do you have any harpoons?"

"Nope."

"Well then," she said, stepping through the opening. "Why didn't you answer the first time I called?"

I shrugged. Queequeg was from a different time and place; Nan couldn't expect him to conform to her kitchen rules.

"I'm too tired to come home from work every day and try to

figure out what fictional character you're playing at. Just answer to your own name. Please."

I looked at Captain Ahab, and he rolled his eyes. Nan and I had gone over this before. I'm only Anna Karenina when I'm out in the garden; Puck when I'm with Cobweb Sneaky Walker, otherwise known as Mr. Douglas, and Huckleberry when I'm particularly mischievous. Queequeg is my almost-every-other-time guy. Unless I'm walking with Archibald. Then I'm Jane. As for Huw, his life was so dismal, it was a mistake even pretending to be him. But Nan didn't care to take all that into consideration and got cross at me when I asked her to recite it back.

"Please," she said again.

I blinked. This was the mountain I was prepared to die on.

Nan sighed and walked out of my room.

Captain Ahab patted my arm, "That'll teach her."

19

After I'd tidied up my sailboat bed, I slipped down to the kitchen. Nan was seated at the chrome table sipping a hot cup of coffee. "What circle was it today?" I asked.

Nan looked up and sighed. "Oh, today wasn't so bad. A five at most."

I nodded. Working at the Happy Valley Druggist plunged Nan into at least one circle of Dante's hell. Anger was one of the better ones. "I bet it was when Mrs. Whitford ran out of the store and started yelling?"

"How did you know?"

"Griggs walked me home this afternoon."

That was all the explanation Nan needed. Mrs. Whitford and Old Lady Griggs were Happy Valley's very own Cain and Abel. Except they weren't related, and neither had the gumption to pummel the other in the head with a rock.

"We will have a different day tomorrow, Celia." Nan blew in her cup. "We'll spend the day baking. Isn't that exciting?"

I shrugged. "That's nothing new. We've baked before."

"True, but this is different. Before we baked for ourselves; tomorrow it will be for others."

I took the chair beside Nan's. "Why would we do that?"

"For a little extra money. Now that I'm paying rent to Mrs. Griggs, I'm stretched pretty thin."

The thought of extra money was tempting, but I couldn't help but worry about Mrs. Jasmine. If Nan took to baking, what would become of her and the Saggy Buns Bakery? I couldn't bear the thought of walking into the bakery and Mrs. Jasmine not pointing to the sign and saying, *"Don't even ask. It happens with age."* She had the voice of a smoker.

Nan noticed my concern. "She'll be fine."

"Who?"

"Mrs. Jasmine. I've already discussed it with her. She's not ready to call it a day, but she doesn't mind if I bake the odd pie and a few pastries. The whole thing has gotten to be too much for her. We'll be doing her a favour."

"What will I do?"

"You'll be my flour sifter. It's almost like spritzing, and you've always loved that. Except sifting is a much more important job. One that can only be trusted to a select few, and not Anna, Huw or Queequeg." She raised her eyebrows. "Who were you when you were my spritzer?"

"I'd rather not say."

"Celia." Nan used her stern voice.

"A faceless proletariat." It made my heart hurt just saying it out loud. "With itchy clothes and only a thin layer of straw to sleep on. The layer filled with mouse poop."

Nan looked put out. "This is the first time I've heard of it."

"That's because I only thought of it now. But you have to admit it kind of fits. A worker bee spritzing until her fingers cramp." I leaned my elbows on the table and thought for a long time. "But would a proletariat be a sifter? It doesn't feel right. Pies and pastries reek of the bourgeoisie."

"I should have never read you that book." Nan got up from the table and put her coffee cup in the sink.

"Which one?" I asked, knowing full well it was an empty threat. I'd overheard her tell Griggs that she wanted me to have a substantial vocabulary, larger than that of any of my naysayers. The ones who poured over my comic strip looking for proof that I'd turn out as poorly as my should-have-been parents. Nan said she wanted my detractors on the back foot before they even opened their mouths.

"Which one?" Nan ran a hand through her hair. "All of them. Every damned one."

The next morning, I tied on one of Nan's old aprons and took my place at her elbow. Nan looked down at me and smiled. "You look tired, my girl."

"I am."

"Didn't you sleep?"

I shook my head. "How could I? I have to be a sifter with no name."

"How about Celia?" Nan finished mixing the pie dough and put it in the fridge to rest.

"That's my everyday name. Have you ever heard of a famous sifter named Celia?"

"Can't say I have."

Nan started peeling the apples she'd collected on the way home from work the day before. Some of our neighbours' trees had yielded more fruit than they could use, and they gave Nan the extras. She tried to peel a whole apple in one long spiraling piece. When she was done, she handed me the peel, and I threw it over my shoulder to see what letter it curled into. It would be the initial of the man I was supposed to marry, according to the game we played. The first throw was a C. I kicked the peel under the table before Nan looked. I didn't want her to think I was to marry Timmy Crybaby-Head.

"Crybaby-Head isn't his last name," Nan said, reading my mind.

I could feel my cheeks grow hot. "I know that." But after two more throws, it was as if my future was carved in granite. C seemed to be the only letter the apple skin was willing to give me. I looked up at Nan. "What's his real last name?"

"Whose?"

"Timmy's."

Nan smiled. "Leach."

"That's not much better, yet it fits."

"Perhaps."

With the apples peeled, Nan rolled the dough, and I became the sifter. But not just any kind of sifter. I picked up the sifter and made my arms go scarecrow straight, as if I didn't have any elbows.

"What are you doing now?"

"I don't know who I is," I said, using my baby voice.

Nan rolled her eyes. "I don't even want to guess."

Standing there with my arms poker straight, twisting my body whenever Nan needed a sift, was harder than it looked. My arms burned and shook a little, but Nan was quiet, and went along as if I was doing nothing out of the ordinary. She hummed, a bit of a smirk where her smile was supposed to be. It wasn't until Griggs came bursting through the door that I got any rest at all.

"Molly!" Griggs bellowed in wonky-eyed wonder, curlers hanging from only one side of her head. She plopped the black scrapbook on the kitchen table, causing flour to billow up around it.

Nan said nothing. She didn't even look in Griggs' direction, probably worried she would increase next month's rent. She wasn't ready for confrontation yet; her bookmark was only at the halfway point in her library book on squatters' rights.

"Molly, have I got something to tell you." That's when Griggs noticed me. "What in land sakes is she doing?"

"Sifting," Nan said.

I nodded.

"With her arms like that? Who in their right mind would sift like that?"

"Celia." Nan crimped the edge of the pie crust with a wet fork. "Though whether she's in her right mind is debatable."

My arms were on fire. I wanted to drop them, but then how could I be the Littlest Christmas Tree? That's who I was now. Old Lady Griggs would understand. Last summer she played the Christmas Tree story for me on her record player. She felt uncomfortable weeping by herself and couldn't bring herself to wait until next Christmas to listen to it again.

Red Skelton was the voice of the tree, and Santa voiced himself. I could almost recite it off by heart. *The time, Christmas Eve. The place, this room. We're making a last-minute check of our lists to be sure we haven't forgotten anyone. We pause for a second and offer a prayer for our neighbours.* We had both cried when two of Santa's reindeer ran into an iron curtain and were knocked out cold.

"Who makes a curtain out of iron?" I had asked Griggs.

"Well, not anyone who cares about children, I'll tell you that much." Griggs pulled me closer, and we listened, hardly breathing. It was one of the few times I didn't worry about one of her bony ribs impaling me. When Santa said he was never asked back for dinner, Griggs and me were inconsolable.

"I've forgotten him too." I put my hands over my face to hide my shame.

Griggs kissed the top of my head. "Me too, child, me too."

That's when Nan walked in. She said we were being ridiculous and that a grown woman shouldn't fall for such cheap propaganda. Griggs said it wasn't cheap. She had paid full price for it at the Happy Valley Druggist, and if Nan didn't believe her, she could ask Mrs. Whitford. Nan said nothing, but she told me to get my things. It was time to go.

I pulled the sifter handle and tried to look as much like a fir tree as I could, but Griggs still didn't recognize me. Forlorn, I said, "I don't know why I is here."

As soon as the words were out of my mouth, Griggs' face lit up. "The Littlest Christmas Tree," she exclaimed with a little jump. She loved that story, especially the way Red Skelton told it. "That man has a gift for the gab," she said. "If I weren't already married, I'd give his wife a run for her money."

Nan finished crimping her crust and started a new pie. "I'm sure you would."

Griggs turned to me. "You look like you're in pain."

I nodded. My arms were going numb. It was like Griggs was reading my mind and knew what to do.

"Pretend your limbs are laden with snow. That way you can put them down until the ice melts."

When Nan had enough of us, she turned to Griggs. "You had something to tell me, Dorigen?"

A look of confusion crossed Griggs' face. "I did, didn't I? But for the life of me I can't remember what it was." She retraced her steps. "I knew it when I got out of bed. That's when I leaned over and shook Mr. Griggs. 'Molly will be furious when she finds out,' I said. Then I made us both coffee and toast. One burnt and one regular. Mr. Griggs likes the burnt kind. Reminds him of his mother's cooking."

She walked around Nan's kitchen as if she were in her own. "I put the breakfast dishes in the sink," she said, miming the action. "Wiped the table, kissed Mr. Griggs." A blush rose in her cheek. "Then I reached for my honeymoon hat. I need it when I have an important engagement such as this." She plopped down in a chrome chair, looking rather pleased with herself.

"And?" Nan prodded.

"And that's all I remember."

"It couldn't have been that important then."

Griggs huffed. "No! It was! I wouldn't have rushed off this morning half done." She pointed to her hair. "My honeymoon hat couldn't even cover my disheveledness."

"Disheveledness?" I raised an eyebrow, knowing she was trying to slip in the dictionary game while Nan was preoccupied. "That's not a real word."

"I don't need a seven-year-old to tell me that. And I don't think that's important now, when you take into consideration my significant news."

"The news you can't remember," Nan reminded her.

"That's neither here nor there." Griggs made to leave, picking up her scrapbook. "I know it was important," she muttered. "Wouldn't have woken Mr. Griggs in the middle of the night if it wasn't. It's on the tip of my tongue." She was almost at the front door when she turned on her heel, her face bright. "Remember when we used to play Pin-the-Tail-on-the-Donkey?"

"How could I forget?"

Griggs didn't acknowledge her. She had taken a seat and was riffling through the scrapbook. "It's somewhere in the Canterberry backstory. After we graduated from high school, but before Walter went to war. Here it is." Griggs jabbed the page.

Young Molly Canterberry struts around town, waving her

behind like a red cape before a bull. She's still absorbed with childhood games, like Pin-the-Tail-on-the-Donkey. And since Farmer Hempel's donkey died from tetanus following the previous year's championship playoff, Molly Canterberry is the most likely stand-in. Molly stomps and strikes out at any soul that dares to accost her. She bruises and bloodies most of her opponents. Few, if any, breach her defences."

Griggs stopped reading and looked up. "Do you remember that, Molly?"

Nan grunted her reply.

Pleased with herself, Griggs flipped to the next page.

But one opponent, little Fanny Shandell, remembers the loss, and as weeks turn to years, she yearns for the day when she can best Molly Canterberry, the best Pin-the-Tail-on-the-Donkey donkey Happy Valley has had the privilege to prick.

Nan stopped what she was doing, her floury hands hovering over the table.

Despite not even qualifying to be poor white trash, Fanny prevails. On a cloudless day, when flags wave and our young men kiss their mother's goodbye, the yearning of Fanny's foul heart turns into a reality. She slips in the shadows, crouches in the alley, and bides her time at the church picnic.

I thought Nan would pass out. She forgot all about her pies and sank into the flour-dusted chair. I didn't even know if she was listening to Griggs anymore.

When most are canoodling, Molly Canterberry and Walter Douglas are lost in their own world. Strolling side by side through the checkered picnic blankets and half-eaten sandwiches, Walter lifts Molly's chin with the tip of a finger. Molly closes her eyes in anticipation. He leans closer. She responds with an ear-splitting shriek. A shriek that reverberates through the streets of Happy Valley.

Fanny Shandell slinks back into the shadows, short a hatpin. She crows, "That's for old time's sake! Remember Pin-the-Tail-on-the-Donkey, Molly Canterberry? As usual, you're the donkey."

"Do you remember that?" Griggs slapped the scrapbook shut.

"I do, but I hadn't realized Oswald Elliot committed it to paper."

"He's sneaky that way. But let's get back to the matter at hand. Do you loathe Fanny as much now as you did then?"

"Why do you ask? I haven't thought about her in almost thirty years."

"Because she's Archibald Quigley's new neighbour. Fanny Shandell is now Fanny Figgler, and she's moved back to Happy Valley!"

"She was the lady at the library that I said looked like a Flo," I chimed in.

Nan shot me a dirty look. "You knew Fanny was back in town and never told me?"

"Well," I back-pedaled, "I kind of did. I told you that Archibald had an annoying neighbour, and you said join the club."

Nan reddened as her gaze darted to Griggs.

Griggs gasped. "No one told me there was a club."

"Besides," I went on. "I didn't know she was a Fanny, only a Mrs. Figgler. And I didn't know she was a famous bum-sticker. Which is kind of surprising, because it sounds like something I'd do."

Tears welled in Nan's eyes, and for the life of me I couldn't figure out why. I'd caused her more grief almost every day of my life.

"Excuse me." Nan stepped into the bathroom and shut the door.

After an unbearable silence, Griggs leaned closer. "We don't have a lot of time. I'll fill you in as fast as I can. Fanny stuck her hatpin in your Nan's meaty behind up to its hilt. Not only did she interrupt your Nan's first kiss, but your Nan had to suffer the indignity of having Doc Marley remove the hatpin. It was the talk of the town.

"Breaks my heart just thinking about it. Before the church picnic, the way your Nan and Walter gawked at one another, everyone was convinced there'd be a wedding. Never seen your Nan do that with another man before or since. And that Fanny, well, she had a bee in her bonnet. I think she carried a torch for Walter. Easy to see why. He'd been sharing his lunch with her for years. She'd come to school all worn out, with hardly a scrap of bread, and Walter would give her half of whatever he had. So you can understand why she went after your Nan like blue blazes. It wasn't just her loss at Pin-the-Tail-on-the-Donkey; Fanny thought Molly stole Walter from her. She palmed her hatpin, slipped up behind them and jabbed your Nan as hard as she could. And that's not the worst part." Griggs fixed her wonky eye on me.

"What's the worst part?"

"Your Nan and Walter Douglas had words. He said Fanny was simple and Nan shouldn't be so hard on her. Nan said he had a blind spot. They agreed to disagree. And when it was time to see him off, your Nan was too cross to go. He boarded the train and left to fight in Europe, and the only woman waving goodbye was Fanny. I don't think your Nan ever forgave herself for being bad-tempered about such a foolish thing. I hate to say it, but Fanny Figgler is going to worm her way back into your Nan's life, hatpin or no. That mudlark, Celia, is your should-have-been-great aunt."

20

Our baking day went downhill from there. Griggs held up an empty coffee cup, waiting for Nan to fill it, while Nan rolled her pie dough until it was tough enough to make a pair of shoes. They didn't speak or look at one another. And there I was in the middle of it all, bursting with questions, like how was Fanny Figgler my great aunt? Nan had no sisters that I knew of, but what about my should-have-been-grandpa? I took a deep breath. "How come you haven't told me about Aunt Fanny before?"

Nan stilled mid-roll. "Don't call her that."

"What am I supposed to call her?"

"Nothing. Call her nothing. As far as I'm concerned, she stopped existing years ago." Nan's voice was like icy knives.

"That doesn't seem very charitable," I sniffed.

Both of Griggs' eyes were almost bulging out of their sockets. The lazy one was making as much effort as the ambitious one. Her head vibrated, begging me to button my lip. I'd have to have rocks in my head not to see it. That's when disillusionment started to fill me, and I swallowed down my curiosity, for now. My consideration went to my Christmas tree arms. They were burning while my mind was turning to mush under the thought of having another despicable family member. I needed some sort of relief. I began sifting flour just for the fun of it. First on the table, then on my toes. In the end, I'd sifted all the way up my legs and started on my hair.

"Celia," Nan barked, when she saw what I was doing.

I froze.

"What's gotten into you?"

"I can't be a Christmas tree without a dusting of snow." I thought my actions were self-explanatory, but Nan was not of the same mind.

"I don't have time for this," she said, snatching the sifter away.

Griggs tapped the side of her cup with a spoon. "What do you have time for?"

Nan's eyes went wild. She turned on Griggs. "I have time to bake and clean. To work at the drugstore and keep a garden. I have time to raise a granddaughter and volunteer whenever I'm needed. But I don't have time to clean up unnecessary messes or pour coffee for whatever fool crosses that threshold." She jabbed a stiff finger towards the door.

Griggs looked offended. "I'm not just any fool, Molly Canterberry. I'm the fool who's stood by you through thick and thin. Sat up when you waited for a letter—just one word. All those nights worrying about Walter, not knowing if he was dead or alive. And then when Celia came along, I walked the floor with her so you could get a few hours' rest. That's the kind of fool I am."

Nan's shoulders shook as she pulled out her chair and sat down at the kitchen table. She covered her face with her hands and cried.

Griggs and me picked up where Nan left off. The pie shells were all rolled, so we just had to fill them and put on the lids.

When we were finished and popping them into the deepfreeze, Griggs looked down at me. "Did we remember the sugar?"

I shrugged. "Is it important?"

"It won't bode well for Nan's reputation as a baker if we didn't."

"Should we tell her?"

We looked at Nan. She'd finished crying and was sitting in her chrome chair, staring into space.

"We'll tell her if someone complains," Griggs said. "By then, the damage will be done, and she can quit this nonsense."

I nodded. Sifting as the Littlest Christmas Tree had been one of the worse decisions of my life. I should have stayed the faceless proletariat. At least then I'd have normal arms.

Griggs tweaked my cheek. "Why not give your Nan some time to herself? You can come with me to Murray's Haberdashery and help me pick out a new string tie for Mr. Griggs. His is looking rather shabby."

"On the way can we talk about Aunt Fanny," I whispered.

"Even I'm not stupid enough to open that can of worms."

I looked from Nan to Griggs before following her out the door. Shopping with Griggs was more than I'd expected. She didn't stop at her house to tidy up or finish taking out her curlers. We headed straight for the haberdashery. Once there, Griggs couldn't make up her mind about which tie would go best with Mr. Griggs' button eyes. I reminded her that his button eyes were gone—she'd used them to buy Nan's house and foil my should-have-been parents' plot to take it from her—but she didn't care. She said it was for posterior's sake, and that I was too young to understand posteriors. I told her that it was posterity. And if she thought it was posterior, she was behind the times. Griggs stuck out her tongue, and I stuck out mine back. As far as I was concerned, string-tie shopping was a waste of my time, and I told her so.

"What would you rather be doing?" Griggs snapped. "Christmas tree arm sifting?"

The contempt in her voice riled me, and I wasn't speaking to her by the time we got back to Nan's. But that didn't stop the old bat from speaking to me.

The kitchen was the way we'd left it, except for one thing—Nan wasn't there. "She must be having a lie-down," Griggs said. "Tell her I'll check in on her tomorrow."

I looked at her with withering disdain. After Griggs left, I cleaned the kitchen the best I could. I swept up the flour and put it back in the bin, because waste not, want not. Then I filled the sink with soapy water and began the washing up. There was hardly any difference between the washed and unwashed dishes, but who was I to judge? If a dish didn't want to get clean, I wasn't going to make it.

"Celia," Nan said, coming up behind me. "I don't think you should accompany Archibald home from school anymore."

"Why not?" I asked, forgetting all about my aching Christmas tree arms. Not accompanying Archibald was almost as bad as having to marry Timmy Crybaby-Head.

"I don't trust her new neighbours."

She couldn't even say their names. To me, that seemed an easy fix. "Why don't you have them over for Sunday lunch? The bum sticking happened so long ago, and like you always say, it's water under the bridge."

"Not this time." Nan went white as her threadbare sheets. "This is not the kind of water that a bridge can cross."

That didn't make any sense to me. "Is it because Fanny Figgler is my should-have-been great aunt? And she hasn't even breathed a word of kindness in my direction?"

"That's exactly who I mean. There's bad blood between Fanny and I. And no amount of Sunday lunches can traverse that divide. Members of that family have caused me more pain than I can express, and I'm not going to give them the opportunity to drink from that well again."

I thought for a minute. There had to be a way of changing Nan's mind. If Archibald and me didn't shake our heads at that mantel clock at least once a day, all hell would break loose. "What about if we never talk to Fanny Figgler again?"

"No dice, kiddo." Nan put on her apron before laying her hand on my cheek.

"What if I take Griggs with me? Griggs will keep her away. She has that effect on most people."

"You can't expect Mrs. Griggs to traipse all over town after you and Archibald."

"She wouldn't mind."

"That's the part that worries me. No telling what that woman might do."

I could feel my eyes filling with tears. "My should-have-been parents aren't enough? Now Archibald has to be my used-to-be friend?" I was sobbing so hard that my voice came out in jerks.

Nan dropped to her knees and pulled me onto her lap. "I don't know what to say, sweet pea. I'm sorry, but that's the way it has to be."

21

The next morning, Griggs came bursting through the door, same as she'd done the day before. "You're not going to believe this," she said, slapping the Happy Valley Journal on Nan's chrome table. "Oswald Elliot has gone too far this time."

Nan and me bent over the paper, scanning it from left to right. And there it was for the world to see: Oswald Elliot had put his pen to paper and finally captured the essence of Griggs.

Nan straightened and rubbed her lower back. "You've always wanted to make it into the paper, Dorigen."

"Not like this." Griggs slapped the page with the back of her hand. "It's ludicrous."

I looked from Nan to Griggs. Neither was budging. Nan's life had been splashed on the pages of the Happy Valley Journal since the day I was born, and most of the time it wasn't very flattering. Now it was Griggs' turn. To me, it didn't seem too bad. She was strolling down Main Street; me tugging on her arm. My Dick and Jane reader head had been exchanged for a perfect replica of Griggs' handbag. Seemed reasonable to me; after all, we'd been shopping at the haberdashery. On the bright side, I was wearing clothes, and I wasn't destroying anything.

Griggs was the discombobulated one. Her hair, what little there was of it, was partly up in curlers—curlers that were the bodies of dead rodents. Think Wilma Flintstone from the wrong side of the tracks. And she was panhandling with her honeymoon hat. In the background, Mrs. Whitford stood shoulder to shoulder with the newest member of the Ladies of the Perpetual Indigence Society: Mrs. Fanny Figgler.

"Did you read what it says?" Griggs was practically vibrating. In her Agnes Obermeyer voice, she mocked Oswald's script. *"On a pleasant September afternoon, when children roam the streets and birds flit from tree to tree, a hag slips into their midst."* Griggs tightened her lips. *"She's always been there, lurking on the edge of society; a stand-in for any beastly nightmare. But on this day, this day of unlimited potential, she ventures farther afield. Some see her lurking on street corners, others skulking in the alleys. But regardless of where the fiend is spotted, Happy Valley's Main Street will never be the same. And not just because of her foul presence, but because of her marauding young ingenue, the bookish little Canterberry troll. Together they have made Happy Valley a far sorrier place. Some might even say god-forsaken."*

When Griggs finished, Nan handed her a tissue. "What did you two do?"

"What do you mean, what did we do? We left you in peace and slipped downtown to buy Mr. Griggs a new string tie. Nothing worth this libelous codswallop."

I nodded. "Griggs dropped a quarter though."

"A penny saved is a penny earned," Griggs interrupted.

Nan's eyes were glazing over. "So what does this have to do with a quarter?"

"Twenty-five pennies," I said.

"Precisely."

Nan's brows knit together as she slapped the strip with the back of her hand. "All this for a dropped quarter?"

"My thoughts exactly." Griggs balled up her hands into fists. "When I catch Oswald Elliot, I'll give him a beastly nightmare. That's what I'll do."

"The quarter rolled under Mrs. Whitford's convertible," I explained, taking a deep breath. "It was muddy, and Griggs didn't feel like slithering under the car to get it. She said if I went, Mrs. Whitford might think I was bleeding her brakes. Which would be okay if no one was looking. But if not, Mrs. Whitford might just hop in and drive over my head. But I told Griggs that wasn't likely. That Main Street was too busy, and Mr. Whitford wouldn't want to lose any business because of all the blood. So Griggs did the next best thing. She grabbed Oswald Elliot and told him to fetch her quarter or she'd give him a wedgie. Without even questioning her, he fetched it."

"Mystery solved," Nan said, handing Griggs another tissue.

"But look at my head!"

"At least your head isn't seasonal."

"Anything would be better than how he drew me," Griggs blubbered. "All my life I've done my best to live an upright existence, avoid controversy and keep to myself. And now I find myself in the middle of Celia's comic strip."

"You should have been more careful about what you wished for."

"I didn't wish for this. Celia leading me around like her hell hound."

I looked closer at the strip. She was right, but then again, so was Oswald Elliot. Griggs was my fire and brimstone pet.

"I wanted to be like Dr. Dafoe," Griggs went on. "Save Happy Valley's only abandoned child."

"That's me," I said.

"The way you two go on," Nan snapped. "Celia wasn't abandoned. She's mine. She's always been mine, from the day she was born."

"Potato, patato." Griggs rubbed her temples with the palms of her hands. "Attitudes like that won't sell papers! Can you imagine an article entitled, *Baby Girl not Abandoned at Hospital,* or *Odd Child Raised by Loving Grandmother.* Where's the je ne sais quoi in that? How many of those novels you love so much would have sold a single copy if that was their premise?" Griggs tapped her foot as she waited for an answer. "Conflict sells, Molly!"

"This is not a fairy tale, a novel, or some made up scenario," Nan said through clenched teeth. "This is real life."

"Don't you think I know that? This is no storybook; it's a comic strip."

Nan threw her arms in the air.

"As I was saying," Griggs continued, "I wanted to be like Dr. Dafoe and take you away as he did the Dionne Quints. Keep you fenced up, riding a tricycle and smiling for strangers." She looked down at me. "Doesn't that sound like fun?"

I was speechless.

"The entire world would have rested easier," Griggs went on, "just knowing I walked the earth. I'd have inspired, I'd have motivated, I'd have transformed. But according to Oswald's depiction, the only thing I do is incite."

"And nauseate. Don't forget about that," I said, pointing to the panel where Mayor Forde was throwing up in the alley.

22

At Monday morning recess, Archibald and me were conferring by the swing set when Timmy Crybaby-Head came running over. "We're not going to let any more air out of Miss Dobbs' tires," I told him, before turning my back. "And there's no use hanging around, because I'm not changing my mind."

Archibald watched him from over my shoulder. "He's still there."

I was getting frustrated. Now that I couldn't accompany Archibald home anymore, this was our only time together, and I didn't want to waste it on some stupid boy. "Go away, Timmy."

"I think he's going to cry." Archibald's eyes were blinking away empathy tears. She'd always had a soft spot for Timmy. She said it wasn't his fault he had a leaky bladder. He was born that way.

"Ok," I relented, turning around to look at him. "Maybe we'll let some air out at lunchtime." But by the way Crybaby-Head wheezed, I knew he wasn't buying it. I wondered how he heard about me throwing apple peels over my shoulder to find out the initial of my future husband. "It could have been half an

S," I said, "and Nan says your real last name is Leach. It didn't look like an L, so don't even try to hold my hand." Then I gave him the death glare. The one Captain Ahab taught me when we weren't harpooning passersby.

Crybaby-Head looked like he was going to be sick. "I don't want to marry you. That's not why I'm here." I was sure I saw him flex his butt cheeks so he didn't dribble in his pants.

"Why are you here then?"

Timmy pointed to the fence that divided the penitentiary yard from the school playground. "Your father wants to talk to you."

At his words, I was sure I could hear Archibald's Prague clock strike the hour. I shook my head.

Archibald grabbed my trembling hand. "No, he doesn't," she said.

"Yes, he does. And he says if you don't come over, he's going to sic your mom on your Nan."

I could feel myself heat up, but not with angry heat. No, this was the kind that made my sight go all blotchy and made sounds seem far away. I grabbed Archibald's shirt and leaned on her. "I need to sit down."

"He's says if you don't come before the last bell, you'll be sorry." After sticking out his tongue, Crybaby-Head skipped away as if he had bells on his shoes.

"I'm already sorry," I said, before everything went dark.

After Timmy's pronouncement, I could hardly control my thoughts. During gym class I wandered around aimlessly, making my team lose at prisoner's base. Usually I was the best tagger. My disappointment was complete.

It wasn't until lunch hour that Archibald and me made a plan. "We need to keep you safe," Archibald said.

"How?"

She scanned the playground and made a beeline to a clover

patch. Why didn't I think of that? We spent the rest of the lunch hour looking for a four-leaf clover. Something I could put in my pocket as a lucky charm. But no matter how hard we looked, we couldn't find one. Archibald plucked a regular three-leafed one and stuck on an extra petal with a bit of spit.

"That's not the same," I said.

"I know." She stood and brushed herself off. "But it's all we have. And besides, your dad won't know the difference. My mom said he didn't even graduate from elementary school."

The bell rang, and I put the spit-stuck clover in my pocket. "Maybe it will be enough."

"Maybe." Archibald let out a deep breath and followed me back into the school.

All through U.S.S.R I stared out the window. Miss Dobbs had started feeding the birds again. I think she missed seeing Oswald Elliot's terrified face peeking over the sill. There were a few sparrows partaking, but no Oswald Elliot. He must have not been peckish. That's when Miss Dobbs slapped my desk with her ruler. "Celia Canterberry," she said. "Do you think you're too good for USSR?"

I shook my head.

"Then why haven't you opened your reader?"

I glanced down at the book on my desk, the one she insisted I read, and without opening it I recited, *Dick. Look, look. Oh, look. Jane. See, see. See Jane. Oh, Jane. Look, look, look. Oh, oh, oh. Oh, see. Oh, see Jane. Funny, funny Jane.*

Miss Dobbs picked up the reader and flipped it open. Her face shrivelled like an apple head doll. "Memorizing isn't reading." She looked at Archibald, slapping the yardstick on her desk.

"Did you help her with this?"

Archibald shook her head.

She turned to Crybaby-Head, slapping the yardstick. "Did you?"

He almost melted in his seat. I slowly lifted my shoes off the linoleum, just in case.

Miss Dobbs moved on. Down one row and up the next she clipped through the classroom, slapping her yardstick and asking the same question. When no one admitted to helping me, she said we'd all have to stay in for recess, so she could sort things out. "Except for Eugenia Whitford, that is." Miss Dobbs smiled and handed Eugenia another muffin. "Unlike the rest of you, Eugenia never disappoints."

Archibald flopped over in her desk and started to wail. Apparently, she'd never been a disappointment before. The sound was getting on my nerves.

It was too much. "I can't," I blurted out. "I have to go to the penitentiary fence and see my should-have-been pa. If I don't, he'll send my should-have-been ma, with her greasy hair wrapped in Nan's peacock scarf, after my Nan."

"And would that be so bad? A family get-together might be just what the doctor ordered." Miss Dobbs sounded as pleased as I'd ever heard her. She didn't look like an apple head doll anymore, she looked like the cat that had gotten the cream.

23

As soon as Miss Dobbs dismissed us at the last bell, Archibald and me ran to the penitentiary fence and looked into the yard. There was no one there. It was empty. No one dragging tin cups across the chain-link fence. No one betting against children's foot races. No one haranguing the recess supervisor or wolf-whistling and saying things that kids shouldn't hear. Griggs said the teachers didn't mind the dirty talk though, because of the danger pay. There were just a few Styrofoam coffee cups blowing about like tumbleweeds in an old western.

"What do I do?" I asked Archibald.

"I don't know."

I pushed my face into the fence and closed my eyes, trying as hard as I could to bewitch my should-have-been out of thin air. I twitched my nose.

"What are you doing?" Archibald looked like she was going to throw up.

"Magicking him."

"I wouldn't do that if I were you. I saw Deadbeat Joe Jr.'s

father pee on it at recess. I think he was trying to spell his name, like he does in the snow."

It figured. Deadbeat Joe Jr.'s father was always peeing on something. I pulled back, and felt the yellow stickiness of it dry to my skin, the droplets welding themselves to my very soul. This was the worst day of grade two so far.

First, my should-have-been wanted to talk to me, then stood me up.

Second, Timmy Crybaby-Head had squeezed the truth out of me—we were destined to marry.

Third, Miss Dobbs kept the entire class in at recess because I knew how to read.

Fourth, I had a pee-soaked face.

And fifth, I wasn't an accompanier anymore.

It couldn't get any worse.

I squeezed Archibald's hand. How could I tell her? I was the only good thing in her life.

But then Archibald blundered into the devastation all on her own. "Want to accompany me home?" she asked.

I looked in the direction of Nan's house, not even brave enough to look her in the face. "I can't. Nan won't let me." I knew Archibald was about to cry; I didn't have to see her to know that. I ripped off the piece of toilet paper stuck to my shoe and handed it to her. She slapped it away.

A whiny voice intruded. "I can. I'll accompany you, Archibald."

Archibald and me turned around. It was Eugenia Whitford. The fancy-dancy troll had been spying on us.

"No one asked you," I said.

Eugenia's wide eyes blinked hard. "Miss Dobbs said it would be a good idea. That I should try to make friends."

I wanted to kick her in the teeth, but Archibald got all

mushy. She looked from me to Eugenia, and I knew her brain was sparking. She smiled. "If Miss Dobbs thinks it's a good idea, then it probably is."

"Archibald," I snapped. "What's gotten into you?"

She shrugged. "Kindness, I guess." She took Eugenia by the hand. "We should get going. My mom will worry."

They did a little arm swing and giggle. It made me sick. And just when I was about to say something, Eugenia turned and stuck out her tongue. Archibald didn't notice, she was so caught up in the glory of walking arm-in-arm with Miss Dobbs' pet.

In the end, I didn't have a choice, so I followed them all the way to Archibald's house. Nan couldn't get mad at me for that, since I wasn't the one doing the accompanying. I was the lowly tagalong.

As I slipped from one tree to another, observing their progress, I muttered under my breath. They didn't even try to save one earthworm. Archibald was changing right before my very eyes, and it was horrifying. I was still her Jane, faithful to the end, but Archibald's Helen was too healthy for her own good. She wasn't leaning on Jane as her decrepitude demanded.

And Eugenia Whitford was even worse. Who was she supposed to be? From the way her empty eyes lollygagged around their sockets, she was Mr. Rochester's crazy wife, Bertha, that's who. The only thing that eased my misery was that Fanny Figgler was waiting for them on her porch swing. It was like she could smell them coming. I slipped into a thicket of nettles that brushed up against the Figgler's picket fence. No one was going to look for me there.

"Archibald." Fanny waved. "Oh, Archibald."

Archibald and Eugenia stopped in their tracks.

Fanny Figgler stood and started walking towards them. She had all the appeal of last month's leftovers. The kind Nan finds lurking in the back of the fridge with fuzzy mold hiding their true identity. Nan was right. Who in their right mind would want to be related to that?

Fanny cleared her throat. "Where's your funny-looking friend? The one with the changeable head?"

"She's not allowed to accompany me anymore."

"Thank the lord for small mercies. I'm sure your mother will be relieved." Her gaze flitted from Archibald to Eugenia. "But I see you're moving up in the world. Eugenia Whitford. You couldn't ask for a better friend than her." She turned her gaze to Eugenia. "So nice to see you, dear."

Eugenia curtsied and blew Fanny a kiss. What was worse, Fanny Figgler pretended to catch it and put it in her pocket. It was like they'd been practicing in their spare time. If that didn't make Archibald throw up, nothing would.

"We don't want any cookies," Archibald blurted.

"That's good, because I'm not offering any, am I?"

Archibald shrugged.

"I've learnt my lesson. What I want is for you to ask your mother if she needs Skinny to do any odd jobs for her. Can you do that, dear?"

I couldn't hear what Archibald said. Her back was as stiff as a board, and I knew *Jesus Loves Me* was probably bubbling on her lips.

"Honestly, don't be bashful. It's a simple question. Does she want Skinny's help or not? If she doesn't scoop him up, someone else will." She said it like it wasn't a threat, but I knew better.

Archibald gave a stiff nod, and Eugenia blew another kiss before she skipped after Archibald, who had fled into the house across the street.

Fanny Figgler stared after them. "Mark my words, Skinny,"

she said, as he came up behind her and placed a hand on her shoulder. "One day, all of that will be ours."

Skinny turned and smiled. That's when I saw them. Butter-covered teeth like almost every other man in the Happy Valley Penitentiary. All that was missing were prison stripes, a mugshot and an abandoned child.

24

I scratched my itches all the way to Farmer Hempel's. Nan had warned me about nettles. Said that I was to avoid them at all costs, and now I knew why. My skin rose in small welts so sharp a blind man could have read my face like braille. Even with all the scratching, I worried about my penitentiary fence visit. The one I should have had. I wasn't going to allow myself to think of it, but now that I was alone, it pushed itself into the front of my thoughts. And the first thing that came to mind was, what could that greasy-haired man want? It couldn't be good. My should-have-been pa wasn't known for his kindness. And it wasn't like we spoke on a regular basis. In fact, the only time he'd spoken to me was when he was robbing my Nan's house. Not one of my best memories.

And where was my should-have-been ma now? She wasn't in the pen with him, or he couldn't have threatened siccing her on my Nan. Old Lady Griggs had once said my should-have-been ma had no fixed address and could lurk anywhere. The thought made gooseflesh rise on my arms in amongst the nettle welts. With all this swelling, Nan wasn't going to be able to recognize me. I might as well lay down and let the ants carry me away to the land of dead earthworms and discarded children.

But I was too itchy to hold still, so I pressed forward, scanning this way and that for my should-have-been ma. There were so many hiding places along the road to Farmer Hempel's —clumps of willow bushes, tall grass growing wild in the ditch, and boulders that had been rolled to the edges of the field to make fences. Any of these places could mask her scrawny frame. I quickened my pace.

What kind of should-have-been didn't have a fixed address? Even Captain Ahab had a fixed address. If I let him wander around the house, willy-nilly, Nan would have a conniption. When I tried to tell Griggs that Anna Karenina was living in our winter cellar, Nan slammed her coffee cup on the table and said if I was going to spew nonsense, she'd throw Anna and her Russian rubber boots out, lock, stock and barrel. I gasped. Anna would have no fixed address, just like my should-have-been ma. No wonder she got run over by a train.

I scratched, and remembered how Mr. Douglas and Tiberius had saved me from my should-have-beens before. When they had been in my bedroom shaking me down for my birthday money, Mr. Douglas and his mangy cat strolled into the kitchen as easy as pie. The sound of them sent the pair scampering. That gave me an idea.

"Leave me alone," I yelled to the empty air. "Tiberius is my friend. He walks me home from school now. Just because you can't see him doesn't mean he's not here." I didn't want my should-have-been to know that I couldn't get near that cat. It just wasn't that kind of friendship; no hugging or touching, just like with Old Lady Griggs. In my mind's eye I could see Tiberius stand on his hind legs and rub his front paws together, facing down my should-have-been ma. His meowing voice yowling, "Fe fi fo fum, I smell the blood of a should-have-been mom. Be she alive or be she dead, I'll grind her bones to make my bread." I loved Tiberius even more at the thought.

I did a quick scan behind me, but nothing stirred. Not a blade of grass, not a leaf; it was all grasshoppers and dragonflies. I let out a deep breath. My should-have-been ma was off making trouble somewhere else.

Farmer Hempel's was just ahead. And to my surprise, my luck was changing, because lo-and-behold, there was Samwise Gamgee. My steps quickened. In all my visits Sam hadn't stood so close to the fence, and if I stretched I could probably touch him. "Sam," I shouted, as I broke into a run. "It's me, Frodo." With all my shaky-kneed worrying, I'd forgotten about him.

Sam lifted his head and nickered. I looked around. There was no one in sight, so that meant he was nickering at me. "Even though we haven't been formally introduced," I placed my hand through the fence, "I've missed you."

Samwise pawed the ground, but it wasn't the same as when Wild Roan did it. He was saying, "Long time no see."

I took two limp carrots from my lunch box and offered them to him. I'd been saving them since the first day of school for this very occasion. "Oh, Samwise," I said, placing my forehead against his munching velvety nose. "I went to the gates of Mordor today, to meet my should-have-been pa. Except he wasn't there, and neither were you. So I had to go as Jane Eyre and take her best friend Helen, who doesn't even know where Mordor is. She thinks Mordor is something you eat at Christmas. We could have been killed."

I gave myself a good scratch before continuing. "And then Mr. Rochester's wife, crazy Bertha, came bustling over and took away my only friend. Except for you, that is. If no one's told you, Mr. Rochester's wife is in league with Sauron. They have matching bracelets."

Sam took it all in, never interrupting once. I told him about

Miss Dobbs and Oswald Elliot. How they were the star-crossed lovers of Romeo and Juliet. Oswald, doomed to sketch unending comic strips, and Miss Dobbs, doomed to teach children she didn't like. I told him about Fanny Figgler, my great aunt, and her son Skinny, who looked nothing like me. Between them and my should-have-beens, I was filled with bad blood to the brim. But that didn't seem to bother Sam. His twitching ears listened to everything I had to say. About how I feared Archibald would show Eugenia her secret library lair, and how Timmy Crybaby-Head was becoming more appealing by the day. At least Eugenia wouldn't try to snatch him. No one would. And how the Figglers were making the move on Archibald's mom. Making sure the next last name she took matched theirs. "I don't know what to think," I told Sam. "If Mrs. Willoughby marries Skinny, Archibald and me would be cousins. But I don't know if I want to be cousins, now that Eugenia is her accompanier."

Samwise said nothing. But he breathed on me, so I knew he understood. I breathed back, hoping he couldn't smell the pee on my face. My insides let go of all their tightening and squeezing. And I remembered what Nan had said about Sir Winston Churchill. She said he was a gruff old man, but the day he died she couldn't help but shed a tear. She said he may have got some things wrong, but there was one thing he got perfectly right—hat the best thing for the inside of a man was the outside of a horse. Sam breathed on me again, and I felt as if I'd been licked by the sun. Itchy, but licked by the sun all the same.

25

When I got home, I looked in the bathroom mirror. My face was a mess. The only way to hide it was to scrub the bejesus out of it. Make Nan think it was due to exuberance. That's when I heard Griggs storm in. "Have I got a bone to pick with you, Molly Canterberry."

I slipped out of the bathroom to investigate. They didn't even notice me; they were squared off in the porch, sort of. Nan was straightening shoes in the porch closet, which left Griggs to address her behind.

"I ran into Claudette Libby today, and do you know what she told me?"

Nan finished with the shoes before she stood. "Pray tell, what did Claudette Libby tell you?"

"That you took out a book on squatters' rights."

"I take out a lot of books, and none of them are any of your concern."

"This one is! It will take the bread right out of our mouths."

"Honestly Dorigen, the only bread that's been taken is Celia's. And that would be your doing."

They both turned to me, and for the first time noticed my ruined face.

"What happened?" Nan gasped. "You look a fright."

Griggs' gaze moved from the washcloth in my hand to my unfortunate countenance. "Isn't it obvious? An object lesson. Cleanliness isn't next to godliness. Anyone who wants to stand that close to God needs their head examined. It's all fine and dandy when you're sitting in a meadow eating fishes and loaves of bread. But then without hardly a warning the plagues come out. Before you know it, you're knee deep in grasshoppers, and breaking out because of soap allergies."

"Celia's not allergic to soap."

"Someone forgot to tell the soap that."

I knew the jig was up. Nan wasn't buying Griggs' allergy malarkey, so I had to come clean. "I crawled into a pile of nettles by the fence." It sounded innocent enough, although I didn't tell Nan what fence. She'd call that a white lie, but I'd call it an oversight.

"I warned you," Nan grimaced. "Even showed you how to recognize the leaves."

"I know, but it was the best hiding spot."

Griggs was having none of it. "I still think it's the soap."

"You're not helping," Nan said.

"I'm not here to help. I'm here to tell you that if you persist with this squatter's rights nonsense, I'll be forced to charge you furniture rent. Which is sixty dollars a month."

"That's the same amount I pay now."

"Precisely," Griggs said, as she flounced out of the house.

"Hoisted by my own petard." Nan blew out her cheeks as the screen door banged shut, then she turned back to me and shook her head. "The things you get into. Well, sit down and let's see what I can do about this mess." With a cotton ball, she dabbed the blotches with calamine lotion. Her eyebrows furrowed. "Did something happen at school? Why did you need a hiding spot?"

"Archibald and I..."

Nan interrupted before I could finish. "*Archibald and I,* is it? Things are that bad?"

I nodded. "I'm not her accompanier anymore. Eugenia Whitford is."

"Oh, sweet pea, I'm so sorry." Nan was sympathetic until she noticed the kitchen chairs. "Did you do this?"

I shook my head. The chairs were upside down on the table, ready for Nan to scrub the floor. I followed her into the living room. All the chesterfield cushions were piled in the corner. "I didn't do that either," I said, without being asked. "Maybe Griggs was searching for loose change."

Nan grunted. "This day keeps getting weirder and weirder. You know, when I got home from work all the shoes were thrown out of the closet? If I didn't know better..." She set things to right, mumbling the entire time.

After that I followed Nan from room to room, wanting to ask her something but not sure what that something was. I watched her sweep, mop, and dust. And was about to tell her she could be more efficient when she got irritated. "Celia, you can't spend the entire day underfoot."

"Why not? I don't feel like playing on my sailboat bed, Captain Ahab has gas. Anna Karenina is stuck down in the cellar. And I can only be Jane Eyre when..." I flopped down on the chesterfield. "What else am I supposed to do?"

"Use your imagination."

My imagination was all used up. I picked up a framed picture Nan had on the end table. It was Nan when she was young. Her father, who looked a lot like her, with the same chin and thinking eyes, had his arms wrapped around Nan and another girl.

Nan leaned over and smiled. "That's one of my favourite pictures," she said, running the feather duster over the glass. Nan didn't talk much about her family. Whenever I asked, she'd say she was too tired or that it was a long time ago.

"Is that your sister?" I tried not to scratch as I pointed to the bony girl who looked a lot like Ichabod Crane from *The Legend of Sleepy Hollow*.

"I don't have any sisters. You know that Celia."

"Not even Fanny Figgler?"

Nan snorted. "Definitely not. If she were my sister, I'd shoot myself."

I could tell by the way Nan set her jaw that that Pandora's Box wasn't going to be opened. I'd have to ask Old Lady Griggs. "Who is she then?"

Nan sat on the arm of the chesterfield and took the picture from me. "That's Dorigen."

Leaning closer, I looked for the telltale wonky eye. Yup, that was Griggs all right. I gasped.

"Celia, we've talked about this photo before."

"But you've never told me it was Griggs. You said it was you, your father and a neighbour girl."

"Then why would you ask if it was my sister?"

I pointed at Griggs. "If my sister looked like that, I'd call her a neighbour too."

Nan chuckled. "You may have a point." She slid from the arm of the chesterfield to the cushion. "This brings back so many memories," she said, forgetting her frustration with Griggs. "It was the night of the father and daughter dance. Dorigen's father was, how do I put this, indisposed. So mine stepped in. I was a little put out at first, wanting him all to myself, but I think it turned out better that way. She said it was the first time she felt beautiful."

I wanted to ask Nan if there was a second time, but didn't want to interrupt her story.

"That was long before the war, or The Ladies of the Perpetual Indigence Society, and Oswald Elliot wasn't even a gleam in his father's eye."

I waited for Nan to go on, but she was thinking about things she didn't want to talk about. I pointed to my great-grandfather's heavy sweater. "That looks warm."

"It was. I think I still have it somewhere in an attic trunk. Dad wore it every chance he got. Mom made it for him, and it pleased her to see him in it. Once she was gone, he rarely took it off."

"I like the buttons," I said, tracing one with a fingertip. "Reminds me of Mr. Griggs' eyes."

Nan's face went tight. "That's right, I'd forgotten." She spoke slower, as if the memory didn't want to come out of hiding. "Dorigen said none of her buttons worked. She said that she wanted Mr. Griggs to look at her the same way she felt that night. That's when she asked if I'd mind taking two off Dad's old sweater."

"So Griggs bought this house at auction with *your* dad's buttons?"

"It appears so." Nan's words were slow, but I knew her mind was whirling. "But let's keep this under our hats, for now at least."

"Because revenge is a dish best served cold?"

"It is if you cook like Dorigen."

26

The next morning, when I saw the shared fence between the school and penitentiary, my heart banged against my ribs. This was the day I had to see my should-have-been. This was the day he would set his beady eyes on me and flash his butter-covered teeth. I tasted a little throw up at the back of my throat and comforted myself with the fact that it tasted better than Griggs' infamous shepherd's pie. As Nan said, we all had to find comfort where we could.

I played Mother-may-I with myself as I made my way towards the school, only allowing six baby steps at a time. It was a slow and painful process, and by the end I was getting on my own nerves. All the other kids had disappeared at the bell, and I was still inching my way across the playground. That's when I heard it.

"Hey kid, get over here." It was my should-have-been. He didn't even know my first name.

My gaze fell to my shoes.

"You heard me, kid. Don't make me repeat myself."

Everything was going the way Captain Ahab had said it would last night as he twisted off his peg leg and slipped it under my pillow. "There are hard men, and then there are hard men."

"Which one is my should-have-been?" I had asked.

"The former."

When I told Nan at breakfast what the captain had said, she'd rolled her eyes and said, 'Oh, God."

"Hey, kid!" my should-have-been yelled one more time.

Off to the side, men were gathering as Deadbeat Joe Jr.'s father finished swigging from a Styrofoam cup. I worried he was about to spell his name. I sighed, gave up on my game of Mother-may-I, and strolled to the fence like Captain Ahab told me to. "Walk like you don't have a care in the world," he said. "Loose-hipped like a cowboy."

"Did you hurt yourself, kid?" My should-have-been pa seemed concerned about my stride until he got a look at my face. It was still rather welty, and Nan had dabbed it with a fresh coating of calamine lotion before I left the house. "Is that what Audrey did? Hang a lickin' on you for not showing up?"

A light went off in my head. Audrey, my on-the-lamb, should-have-been ma, was the one who'd mussed up the shoes, put the chairs on the kitchen table, and moved the chesterfield cushions. But I wasn't going to tell my should-have-been pa that. Let him stew in his juices, as Griggs would say. I shrugged, and as nonchalantly as I could said, "This is from nettles." As if crawling around in poisonous plants was one of my favourite passtimes.

But instead of throwing him off his game, my should-have-been looked proud. "I remember when I used to do that. A chip off the old block." He motioned to two men standing on either side of him. "The boys didn't believe you were mine. Now there's no denying it. The idiots didn't even recognize me from my very own comic strip."

I bristled.

His head jerked to the right. "Especially Limpy. He lost a tooth trying to prove me wrong." He jerked his head left. "Gimpy, on the other hand, is so gullible he'd believe almost anything. Wouldn't you, Gimpy?" He jabbed the saggy-faced man in the ribs. Besides Limpy's swollen lip, the two were identical. My should-have-been had quite the prison entourage.

"The kid from the comic strip, as I live and breathe." Limpy tried to reach through the wire to touch me.

I took a step back.

"Wouldn't have believed it if I hadn't seen it with my own eyes."

If my should-have-been could be proud of me, I think that was the moment. He ran his tongue over his butter-covered teeth while the twins took me in. "I told them," he said, "that any kid of mine would do anything I asked. Isn't that right, kid?"

I spit, just like Captain Ahab told me to, and moved my head slightly. Not saying no, but not saying yes either.

"That's why I wrote you this here note." My should-have-been held up a hand stained with dirt he'd not even tried to scrub free. Gripped between two grimy fingers was a filthy envelope. "Take it to the mayor's office and I'll call us even." He paused. "For now."

My face lightened. "Is that all you want me to do? Pass a note?"

He snatched it back. "It's for the mayor's eyes only, not that empty-headed secretary of his. Kapeesh?"

My should-have-been pa and his sidekicks chuckled. "What did you think I wanted, kid? A cake with a file in it?"

"Maybe," I said, taking back the envelope.

"The apple doesn't fall far from the tree, I'll tell you that, boys," I heard my should-have-been say as he walked away. "Not far from the tree."

For the rest of the school day, that note almost burnt a hole in my pocket. If Miss Dobbs knew, she'd have ripped it up in front of the class and called it dirty prison contraband. There were rumours she'd done that with Deadbeat Joe Jr. once. Then she made him stand in the corner with a piece of gum on his nose. He missed the spelling test. Joe Jr. didn't mind; he hated spelling. Besides, he said, he had been too dehydrated to study.

———

"Eyes front and hands on desks." Miss Dobbs' black shoe tapped the floor. She spoke to the class, but she was looking at me.

"My eyes are front," I said, laying my hands palms-down on my desk.

"And no talking." She clip-clopped up and down the rows examining our finger nails, her yardstick at the ready. Tomorrow was head lice day, and Miss Dobbs didn't want to be accused of dereliction of duty if one of the local nit pickers found a louse.

"Unhygienic hands lead to lice. And lice lead to ringworm. In this classroom, ringworm won't be tolerated." Miss Dobbs paused in front of my desk. "I don't remember you looking like this yesterday."

"I didn't."

"Well, as long as it's not ringworm, or anything else contagious."

"Nettles," I said.

She snorted, finished her inspection, and took her post at the front of the classroom.

"I have good news. The school has been asked to be part of next month's Happy Valley's Halloween Spooktacular. Our class has been chosen to do a Social Studies project, *Who Are the*

People in Your Neighbourhood? The best project will receive a cash prize."

I almost squealed out loud. If the note from my should-have-been pa wasn't smoldering in my pocket, this would have been the best day in grade two.

"Think about it," Miss Dobbs continued. "Next week we'll divide up into groups."

The after-school bell rang. Archibald and me were out of there like a shot. "I'll be in your group," I said.

Archibald paused before she spoke. "Miss Dobbs was talking about real people, right?"

I nodded.

"Not Anna Karenina or Captain Ahab?"

They're real people too, I wanted to tell Archibald, but she wouldn't understand. Her mother had her own library, but it was full of unread books. "They can't come alive if you don't open the pages," I said, but not loud enough for Archibald to hear.

"It doesn't really matter anyway; Miss Dobbs is the one who is going to divide us." Archibald gave a weak smile.

That's when Eugenia Whitford beat her feet in our direction and grabbed Archibald's hand. "Ready for me to accompany you home?"

Archibald nodded before asking me if I wanted to come.

I touched the note inside my pocket. "I have to go to the mayor's office."

"To the *mayor's* office?" Archibald mouthed the words. Her eyes widened in wonder. She'd been terrified of the mayor ever since I told her he had a rodent living in his oversized belly button. "Do you think it's safe?"

"I can't see why not?"

Eugenia's dull eyes were filling with impatience. "Helen, we must get going," she said, giving me a smug glance. "You know how Mr. Rochester hates it when I'm out in the rain."

"You're right, Jane," Archibald answered, but there was no joy in her voice. She looked like she'd just heard the cock crow for the third time. All the same, though, the words jabbed right into my heart. It was hard to breathe. Who gave Eugenia Whitford the right to be Jane Eyre?

I narrowed my eyes, staring straight at my underage nemesis. "What was Jane's favourite colour?"

Eugenia shrugged.

"Her favourite school teacher? After-school snack?"

"Who cares?" Eugenia tugged on Archibald's hand.

As they walked away, my bottom lip quivered. Eugenia had replaced me as Jane Eyre in Archibald's heart. That pasty-faced interloper was a millstone around my neck. Archibald and I weren't best friends anymore. In fact, we weren't any kind of friends at all.

———

I walked to the mayor's office in a daze. I'd expected more of Archibald. How could she have thought so little of me? Used me like the Kleenex Griggs had slipped under her brassiere strap one too many times. I had been lashed to the sail like the little girl in The Wreck of the Hesperus, and Archibald didn't even pause to watch me go down with the ship. I sniffed down my disillusionment and concentrated on the envelope in my pocket.

The mayor's office was next to the hospital, with only a rosebush and a few dud tulips to divide the boundary. I stood in the parking lot and examined the buildings. It wasn't the hospital I was born in. That one burnt down when Ned, the ambulance driver, crashed the ambulance into a power pole, toppling it straight into the storage room where Morris the janitor kept his still.

I closed my eyes and tried to imagine the first time Griggs showed me the comic strip. The old hospital was three stories, not the single-layered building it was now. But the parking lot, that hadn't changed. In my imagination I conjured the rusty old truck, my should-have-been pa leaning against it, yelling up at a window. My should-have-been ma yelling back. Him telling her to hurry up like she was in some change room trying on a dress. Her, leaning out the window and waving her fists through the air. Griggs had said my beginnings were inauspicious, and the more I thought about it, they probably were.

The town office was a different story. I'd never been there before. There were no comic strips depicting me running down the halls with the mayor's belly button rodent in close pursuit. Not yet, anyway. I pulled open the heavy oak doors and wedged myself through the opening. The sign said the mayor's office was on the second floor. That seemed easy enough. I touched the note in my pocket. What harm could a little note do?

Agnes Obermeyer was seated at her desk when I stepped into the office. "Fancy seeing you here," she said, the same unlit cigarette bobbing on her lip. At least I think it was the same. It was wrinkled and slightly bent in the middle.

"Is Mayor Forde in?"

"Is he ever?" Agnes raised an eyebrow and touched the side of her nose. "But I'm not one to talk. That's not my job. I'm to sit here, answer phones, and look pretty."

"Is that what the mayor told you?"

"The sitting here and answering phones part, looking pretty is my own interpretation."

I took a seat and waited. He'd have to come back sooner or later. Agnes went back to filing her nails and ignoring the phone until it had rung at least ten times. She said if someone wasn't willing to wait, their call wasn't that important and she wasn't of the mind to waste her time.

The clock ticked, marking off the minutes I was doomed to wait. It seemed endless. When the boredom overtook me, I began to swing my legs, pretending they were connected to invisible strings, like my very own twin Pinocchios. It was quite a performance. Each puppet trying to outdo the other in case Geppetto got bored and threw one of them in the fire.

Agnes cleared her throat, and I looked up. "I used to do that," she said, pointing to my legs.

"What?" I asked, a little frightened at how much Agnes Obermeyer and I could be alike.

"Test to see if I had polio." She opened the top drawer of her desk and took out a bottle of fingernail polish. "Frightening, isn't it?"

I nodded.

She painted her nails while my Pinocchio legs did their utmost to worm their way into Geppetto's heart. It was for naught, since he'd fallen asleep. I looked around the room. What to do? What to do? That's when I slipped my hand under the chair to check for gum. Before I hit pay dirt, Agnes tapped the face of her watch.

"He won't be coming now," she said. "It'll be pre-happy hour at the Happy Valley Beer Parlor, and the mayor will want to dust off his favourite stool. I don't think he's missed one happy hour since they elected him into office. Claims if he keeps the men happy, they'll tell their wives which way the wind blows."

I felt like crying. What was I going to tell my should-have-been? He'd lick his butter teeth before sticking his scarecrow arms through the chain-links to rip me limb from limb.

"What did you want the mayor for, anyway?"

I slipped the message out of my pocket. "My should-have-been pa wanted me to give him this."

Agnes looked down at the envelope and opened the bottom desk drawer. "Put it in here."

The drawer was crammed full of paper, envelopes and boxes. I looked at her doubtfully.

"If he's the God-appointed mayor, like he claims he is, he'll know."

I hesitated before adding the envelope to the pile. That's when I heard another strike of

Archibald's Prague clock, signalling my doom.

27

When I stepped through Nan's front door, I could hear Anna whining in the cellar. "I can't deal with you now," I snapped. "I'm barely in the door and you're already complaining."

Nan stepped into view, wiping her hands on a dishtowel. "Who are you talking to?"

"Anna," I replied, using a less snappy voice. I thought Nan would scold me and throw Anna out, lock, stock, and barrel, just like she'd threatened.

"Serves you right for locking her in the cellar."

I wanted to tell Nan that I didn't lock her down there. That she was stowed away during inclement weather. Remind her of the winter Anna Karenina and Captain Ahab bunked together, when neither of us got a moment's rest. While Captain Ahab was battening down the hatches, Anna was reopening them to air things out. The two were at loggerheads, especially Captain Ahab. He'd never had his hair pulled before.

I followed Nan into the kitchen where she was putting the finishing touches on a macaroni and tuna casserole. "You look out of sorts," she said, shutting the oven door. "A penny for your thoughts."

"Which ones?" I wasn't sure any of my thoughts were worth a penny.

"The ones you're selling."

That's when it all came bubbling out. I couldn't help myself. Things had been niggling in the back of my mind ever since my after-school rendezvous. "Remember when the shoes were thrown out of the closet and the chairs were on the table?"

"That happened yesterday. I'm not doddery yet."

"Yesterday, my should-have-been pa told Timmy Crybaby-Head through the fence that if I didn't come to the fence and talk to him, he'd sic my should-have-been ma on you."

Nan's lips went thin. "So you think it was Audrey that was up to no good?"

I nodded.

"Don't you think I know that? She's done it before. It's her way of letting me know she's been here."

"Why didn't you tell me?"

"There was no need for you to worry. And believe you me, I can take care of Audrey." She dabbed my face with fresh calamine lotion. "What else did he say?"

I shrugged. She'd only get mad if I told her about the note. Spending time with Agnes Obermeyer wouldn't be on the top of Nan's list of after class activities either. Besides, the note was already delivered, so what was the point? So I got to what was really bothering me. "He said the apple doesn't fall far from the tree."

The cotton ball hovered in midair. "Do you know what that means?"

"I think so. It means we're the same."

Nan leaned over and put my face between her palms. "Oh, honey." Her voice was firm. "You're no apple, and he's no tree."

After supper, when Nan settled down to re-read Jane Eyre, as she knew it was a favourite of mine, my stomach churned. Even the mention of that four-letter word, Jane, sickened me.

"*There was no possibility of taking a walk that day,*" Nan read. "*We had been wandering, indeed, in the leafless shrubbery an hour in the morning; but since dinner (Mrs. Reed, when there was no company, dined early) the cold winter wind had brought with it clouds so sombre, and a rain so penetrating, that further outdoor exercise was now out of the question.*

I was glad of it: I never liked long walks, especially on chilly afternoons: dreadful to me was the coming home in the raw twilight, with nipped fingers and toes, and a heart saddened by the chidings of Bessie, the nurse, and humbled by the consciousness of my physical inferiority to Eliza, John, and Georgiana Reed."

As Nan licked a finger to turn the page, I burst into tears. "What's got into you?" she said, looking up from the book.

"Archibald and Eugenia," I could hardly go on, "are playing Jane Eyre now. I've been replaced."

"Oh," Nan said.

"And as much as I loved Jane before, I hate her now, seeing Eugenia's face plastered over hers..." I couldn't continue through the sobs.

"I see," Nan said, tossing the book aside. I'd never seen her toss a book before. To her they were sacred things. "I've always found Jane to be a bit of a supercilious little prude myself." She picked up the next book in the pile. "*Tess of the D'Urbervilles, by Thomas Hardy,*" she read, and I sniffed and snuggled closer. "*On an evening in the latter part of May a middle-aged man was walking homeward from Shaston to the village of Marlott, in the adjoining Vale of Blakemore or Blackmoor. The pair of legs that carried him were rickety, and there was a bias in his gait which inclined him somewhat to the left of a straight line. He occasionally gave a smart nod, as if in confirmation of some opinion, though he was not thinking of anything in particular. An empty egg-basket was slung on his arm, the nap of his hat was ruffled, a patch being quite worn away at its brim where his thumb came in taking it off. Presently he was met by an elderly parson astride a gray mare who, as he rode, hummed a wandering tune."*

I closed my eyes, drinking in every word, and swore Archibald would never hear about Tess and her disaster bills.

28

The next day at recess Archibald and Eugenia were whispering. "We're going to play Barbies," Eugenia blurted out when she saw me. "And I only brought two, so you can't play."

Archibald looked down at the doll like I wasn't even there.

"I don't want to play. Nan says Barbies give girls unrealistic expectations. Women's bodies don't look like that."

"I guess you'd know, wouldn't you? My aunt says the girls in your family are built like a brick shithouse." When I didn't respond, Eugenia stuck out her tongue and skipped away with Archibald.

My eyes followed them to the swing set, but my feet stayed put. That's when I started blundering from one group of kids to another, but no one asked me to play. Finally, I came upon Timmy Crybaby-Head bent over, looking at the ground. "Still playing with dead flies?" I asked.

"None of your beeswax." He flung out his arms, so I couldn't see what he was doing.

"Thought I'd join you."

"I don't want you to join me."

"Fine. I'll tell Miss Dobbs that you let the air out of her car tires."

"Did not."

"I saw you with my own eyes, and you won't be able to defend yourself because you were a tree at the time."

Timmy looked horrified, but his body shifted so I could see his playmates.

"How do you tell them apart?" I asked.

"I can't, they're faceless...." He paused, as if trying to conjure up the word. His face brightened. "It's a fancy word for worker bees."

"Proletariats," I offered.

He nodded emphatically. "Exactly."

Between Archibald choosing Eugenia, and Timmy almost saying proletariats, my world felt like it was going to shatter. I sat through USSR flipping through my reader, hoping its boredom would lull me. I watched Archibald's back as she leaned forward to whisper in Eugenia's ear. When Miss Dobbs patted her on the head, Archibald looked up at her like Pavlov's dog. I averted my eyes. That's when my gaze landed on Timmy Crybaby-Head. He whimpered at Miss Dobbs' approach, and to my utter shame I felt a solidarity with him. It was all I could do not to burst into tears.

I walked home in a daze. Those words, that Timmy almost said, echoed through my head, *faceless proletariats*. Those were my words. How could marvelous words like those float around in that empty melon?

When I got home, I plunked down at the kitchen table. Nan plunked down beside me, watching me for a long time. "Out with it," she finally said.

I could hardly bring myself to say it. Nan's fingers drummed the table. "Timmy Crybaby-Head knows what a faceless proletariat is."

"Are you sure?" Nan was suspicious, she knew as well as I did that Timmy's vocabulary rarely passed three syllables.

"That's what he called the dead flies he plays with."

"That's odd."

I wasn't sure if Nan was talking about the flies or the word. "What if it's a sign of things to come? What if the apple peels were right?"

Nan ruffled my hair. "You are an odd duck."

"That's what everyone calls Timmy." If Nan said anything after that, I didn't hear her. I was inconsolable.

It took Nan till the middle of the night to find the words. I'd been singing Jesus Loves Me, just like Archibald did that night in Farmer Hempel's cow pasture, and my snot bubbles were two steamboats apart. After two hours on the same verse, Nan came stumbling in my bedroom door, looking like she hadn't slept in an age.

"Enough is enough," she said, taking her spot at the edge of my bed. "I can't watch you disappear before my eyes." Her voice was soft, as if it had given up. "There will always be a Figgler or Shandell, no matter how much I hope to the contrary. The only thing to do is face them head on. I'll talk to Fanny in the morning. Let her know she has to stay away from you when you accompany Archibald home. She's the adult, not you, and you shouldn't have to change your habits just because she's moved back here. And I'll let her know that you're my girl, and she shouldn't get any ideas about trying to take you away from me. Even if she is your great aunt."

I sniffed and wiped my nose down the side of her nightdress. "Are you sure?"

"Of course I'm sure." She pulled back and lifted my face up to look directly into my eyes. "You've always been mine, even when I didn't know it."

29

After school the next day, I found Nan in the kitchen. She gazed into the fridge. "You up for a fried bologna sandwich?"

I licked my lips. Nan only fried bologna when she was in a hurry. All day I'd been imagining confronting Fanny Figgler and getting my old life back. Fanny wouldn't know what hit her. "What are you going to say?"

Nan dipped her bread into ketchup. "To tell you the truth, I'm not sure. I haven't seen Fanny in years, and when we last met, it didn't go well."

"Did you save the hatpin? The one she stuck you with."

"Of course not. You say the strangest things."

"I don't think it's strange. I've heard that when some soldiers get shot, sometimes they save the bullets and make them into a pendant." That very thought pleased me to no end. I'd have bragged at school. Made everyone envious of my Nan and her hatpin necklace. How many kids have grandmothers that have been stabbed in the bum? I looked at her in wonder.

"Well, I'm not a soldier," Nan snapped.

I sneaked a lick of my ketchup-covered plate. "Griggs says

love is a battlefield. Don't you wish you had that hatpin now? You could tell Fanny Figgler to stick it where the sun don't shine."

Nan tried to hide her smile, but I could see she was more pleased than shocked by my suggestion.

When we finished, we put the dirty dishes in the sink without washing up. That could wait until later, Nan said. She had bigger fish to fry. And with a final check in the bathroom mirror, Nan and me were out the front door. The weather was unusually hot for September, and Nan was getting armpit stains before we'd gotten to the end of the block. "Do you want to take the shortcut through Farmer Hempel's pasture?" I asked.

"I don't think that would be wise. Remember that wild roan?"

How could I not? That cow was the bane of my existence. Still, I thought it might be prudent. "If we don't," I pointed to Nan's crescent moons of perspiration, "you'll be swimming in that shirt."

Nan tucked her arms in closer to her sides. "Celia, do you have to comment on everything?"

I knew by her tone I wasn't expected to answer.

The closer we got to the Figglers, the more Nan muttered. I knew better than to interrupt. She was practicing what she would say, just like I had with Captain Ahab. "Queequeg," Captain Ahab said, stretching and scratching himself awake. "She's an old woman. Don't expect too much of her."

I nodded.

"You won't know if she's got it in her until she knows she's got it in her."

I looked up at Captain Ahab; he was the wisest one-legged man I knew.

"Queequeg, do you have any harpoons on you?"

"Nan made me throw them away."

"She'll regret that decision."

There were no truer words.

As Nan and me trotted across Happy Valley, Captain Ahab's words slipped in and out of my thoughts. If he was right, Nan and me were defenseless. If he was wrong, I was worrying about the harmless musings of a drunken sailor. But how was I to know which was which? I grabbed hold of Nan's hand. "Be Countess Vronsky," I whispered.

Nan stopped mid-stride and looked down at me. "Pardon me?"

"Be Countess Vronsky," I said, a little louder.

She chewed over my words, then nodded grimly. "Don't worry, I intend to."

After that, Nan's shoulders braced and her chin set. I almost felt sorry for Fanny Figgler.

Nan pressed on down Main Street. She hardly waved and didn't stop for idle chitchat. It was like she was afraid she'd lose her nerve. Once jabbed, twice shy. I did my best to keep up. When we passed Mrs. Whit-ford and the Happy Valley Druggist, Nan barely grunted in her direction. It seemed to unsettle Mrs. Whitford. She looked at her reflection in the store window before withdrawing inside. Through the glass, I heard her call to her husband. "Do I have something in my teeth?"

The only thing that was missing was Old Lady Griggs. I wished she was with us. Just like the Three Musketeers, striding down Main Street in our cavalier boots, our capes snapping in the breeze. If Archibald wanted, I'd let her join. She could be called Afterthought, the musketeer who never was. The four of us could storm Mayor Forde's office and slash Oswald Elliot's bike tires. Whatever struck our fancy, as long as we left Eugenia Whitford in the dust. In time, Archibald would even get used to

Griggs' lazy eye and learn to think of it as an entertaining bonus.

When we reached Fanny's house, Nan wasn't even out of breath. She looked down at me and whispered, "Elbow's out Celia, there be harpies." Then she banged open the front gate and marched right up to the front door. She was about to knock when Fanny Figgler came toddling around the corner holding a taped broom. I recognized it immediately.

If there had ever been niceness in Fanny Figgler, it drained from her now. "I wasn't expecting company."

"We're not company," Nan said archly, using the royal *we*. She was Countess Vronsky, imperious to the core. I imagined her in long white gloves up to the elbows.

Fanny sniffed. "What are you then?"

I wanted to tell her I was Anna Karenina, but sadly that part of me was locked down in a cellar counting spiders. And since Griggs was nowhere in sight, I couldn't be Porthos, my favourite musketeer. Queequeg would just confuse her. I would have to be Celia, plain old Celia. As disappointed as I was, I reached up and took Countess Vronsky's hand, and that of my very own Nan.

Nan got straight to the point. "I had hoped Dorigen was wrong, but I see she wasn't."

"And what do I care what Cockeye thinks?"

Nan narrowed her eyes. "I haven't heard her called that for years. It wasn't kind then, and it's not kind now. And you should care. Dorigen can be quite a handful, but that's not why I've come. Nor have I come to welcome you back into the community. In fact, when you left I thought it was a godsend. Felt a weight lift. What I've come for is to set a few non-negotiable boundaries."

"And if I don't want to negotiate?"

"That's not up for negotiation. Weren't you listening?"

Fanny Figgler was getting lost in Nan's words. I could see it on her face. She fingered the tape on the broom handle, and I knew she was regretting the mend. "And who decided that?"

Nan stepped into Fanny. All those years of harboring a hatpin scar spewed out of her. "Who decided? Me. I decide."

Fanny's lip quivered. "I think Enid would disagree. The Ladies of the Perpetual Indigence Society have welcomed me with open arms."

"Enid, is it? She must think you're a prize. But I doubt Enid Whitford realizes your history or remembers who you were before you were a Figgler. And when she's reminded, she'll unwelcome you just as fast as she welcomed you." Nan paused and breathed in another dose of Countess Vronsky. "But that's not why I've come today. I've come to give you a warning. To tell you to stay away from my Celia."

"And why would I do that?"

"So I keep your secrets. Every sordid one."

Fanny scoffed. "Oh, Enid wouldn't mind that I pricked you with a pin. She might even encourage me to do it again."

"Perhaps, but that's not the only secret you've been keeping." Nan jutted out her chin. "If I remember right, Fanny Shandell, you held up the Happy Valley Bank when you were barely thirteen. You let out Farmer Hempel's cattle, causing a stampede down Main Street. And you set the Catholic Church alight, on Christmas Eve, no less."

"Set the church on fire? St. Drogo's?" The little Christmas tree in me was incensed; I could have been in there. That was almost as bad as an iron curtain. A tiny, shadowy part of me admired Mrs. Figgler's rap sheet, but the saucy way she talked back to Nan made me mad. I wound up a good one and kicked Fanny Figgler right in the shin. She howled. Nan put her hands on my shoulders to still me.

"Setting a church on fire is child's play." Fanny's voice grew chilly with icicles. "And if you want to talk of secrets, let's talk about Walter's."

"This is neither the time nor the place," Nan stuttered.

"You picked it." Fanny stepped closer. "I'm an aggrieved widow, remember? Whereas you're a brazen hussy, claiming you didn't entice my brother, what is it? Almost thirty years ago? Who'd believe that nonsense? Just look at you, frumpy as ever, whereas my brother was a real head turner. It's one of the things I'm going to correct. Clear our good Shandell name. More than likely, you lured the poor man over to make Walter jealous. You wanted to get his attention as soon as he stepped off the troop train."

I looked from Fanny to Nan. Nan's face was white, and it looked like her soul was melting.

Fanny picked at the tape on her broom handle. "It was there in the comic strip, remember? You crumpled on the floor, Walter comforting you. But we both know what really happened. Don't we?" Her gaze burrowed into Nan's. "And the thing that's had me scratching my head all these years is that Brian, my beloved brother, hasn't been seen since. Not hide nor hair. And from what I hear, neither has Walter's Luger."

Nan placed her hands on my shoulders and pulled me close. When she spoke, her voice cracked. "This is not about Walter and your twisted delusions. I'm here for Celia. I want you to stay clear of her. Don't look at her, don't talk to her, don't even think about her. For that matter, stay clear of both of us."

"Do you really think I want anything to do with that child?" Fanny Figgler swung the broom in my direction.

That's when Nan lost her mind. She slipped from being Countess Vronsky to Eliza Doolittle, almost knocking me to the ground in the process. In one fell swoop, Nan catapulted over me and grabbed on to Fanny Figgler's hair with both hands.

That old bum-sticker never saw it coming.

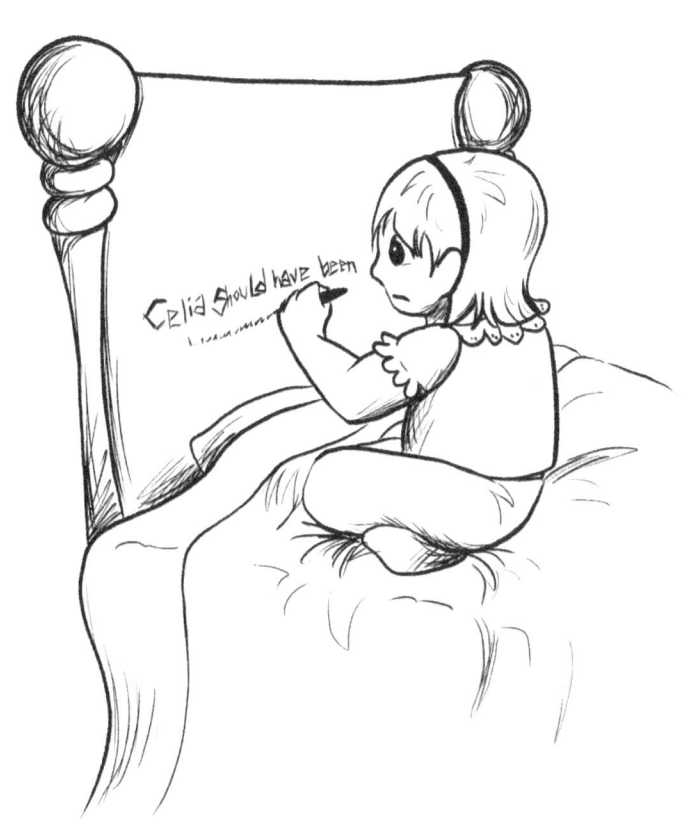

30

When Nan tucked me in that night, she wasn't herself. She did everything she usually did, including saying my prayers with me. *Matthew, Mark, Luke and John, bless the bed that I lie on. Four corners to my bed, four angels round my head. One to watch and one to pray, and two to bear my soul away.* But her voice was far away and unconvincing. As soon as she was out of the room and safely down the hall, I took the flashlight I stowed from under my pillow. Then on my headboard, under where I'd carved 'Celia should-have-been,' I began my list. This time I used a ballpoint pen instead of Nan's best butter knife, so it didn't look like the work of the midnight drifter. (He was the man who broke into my Nan's house a long time ago and hurt her before Walter could stop him. His name was Brian, and he was Fanny Figgler's brother.)

1. Get Nan's house back.
2. Find a new best friend.
3. What's a Luger?
4. What was on my should-have-been's note?
5. Stop Skinny from marrying Mrs. Willoughby, and sic him on Miss Dobbs.

I paused and tapped a fingernail on my teeth before writing the rest of my list. The next ones were the hardest two, no matter what Nan told me.

6. Am I an apple?

7. Is she my forever Nan?

I looked over my list. I had a lot of work to do.

31

Nan was still smarting from her confrontation with Fanny Figgler. She didn't tell me, but she didn't have to. At first it was in her eyes and the way she held her shoulders, then in the way she plunked down the dishes on the breakfast table. And by the time she got back from stocking shelves at the Happy Valley Druggist, she was almost coming out of her skin. It was times like this she seemed most inspired by Jack LaLanne. He had his own exercise show on the CBC. Griggs said if any man was worth getting sweated up with, it was him. Nan knew his routines off by heart, and as soon as she stepped through the door she took hold of a kitchen chair and started stretching. I snuck up behind her, spritzing when she looked like she was about to overheat. It didn't help.

"Cheer up," I said. "Things will look better tomorrow."

"And why is that?" Nan panted as she counted out fifty jumping jacks.

I didn't have a good answer. When she was done, she filled the kitchen sink with water and started on the neglected breakfast dishes. I stood beside her and stirred the bubbles with a spoon, trying to make a little whirlpool.

"Is it the Fowl Supper?" I asked. Nan had circled the date on the calendar months ago. The day the entire town got together at the hall, ladies in the kitchen making turkey, stuffing, mashed potatoes and jelly salads, men in the hall complaining about how hard they worked. Griggs was in charge of cutting pickles. The other proletariats knew it was a risk giving her a knife, but what else could they do, considering her cooking acumen? All this to celebrate the last of the fall harvest being brought in.

We never used to go. Nan was always fearful that someone would tell me about my comic strip, which I wasn't supposed to know about. But now that the cat was out of the bag, thanks to Griggs, we could attend without fear. Well, without *that* fear anyway. Nan could, once again, be a faceless proletariat, working in the kitchen shoulder to shoulder with all the other worker bees. Except The Ladies of the Perpetual Indigence Society. They didn't work; they just walked around with their checklists, making sure everything was up to their standards.

Nan said she used to attend before I was born. She and Griggs and Farmer Hempel's wife would send Mrs. Whitford into a tizzy. They kept her running back and forth, making sure they were doing their work and not visiting too much. Mr. Griggs was always stuffed into a corner out of the way, propped up and hunkered down at the same time. He gave Mrs. Whitford the willies. She said it made her skin crawl, the way his button eyes followed her around the room. On the contrary, Nan said, the attention put a spring in her step.

Now she dithered at the thought. "Maybe we shouldn't go, Celia. I don't think I can face anyone. With the rumours, and pulling Fanny's hair like that. What will people think of me if she tells them?"

I shrugged. "Archibald and I used to pull each other's hair

all the time. I think it made us closer." I paused. "Until it didn't."

"Well, that's you and Archibald. We're full-grown women."

"You're going to have to face everyone sooner or later."

Nan gave a curt nod. "You're right," she said, although I barely heard her. She finished the dishes and drained the sink. That's when I asked her if Mr. Douglas would come. I never called him Sneaky Walker anymore, not since he helped Nan put her potato sacks in the cellar. Watching the way they looked at each other, I knew he was my could-have-been grandpa.

"I don't know if he's coming, Celia," she said. "Large crowds bother him. With all the loud voices and banging, I doubt it. I used to put a plate out for him on the back step and he'd eat under the ancient elm at the back of the lot. I'd join him from time to time. We'd drink lemonade and listen to everyone else visit. It's been so long. I don't know if anyone's shown him that courtesy since you've been born. But if they haven't, I'll start again tomorrow night."

"Do you leave one out for Tiberius too?"

"No, he wasn't around then, but I suppose I should. I'll save him the neck. Cats like the neck. I'll have to do it when Mrs. Whitford isn't looking. She objected to me feeding Walter, so she'll certainly protest if she catches me feeding his cat."

"Do you care?"

"Oh no. If there is anything I'm looking forward to, it's Mrs. Whitford's objections."

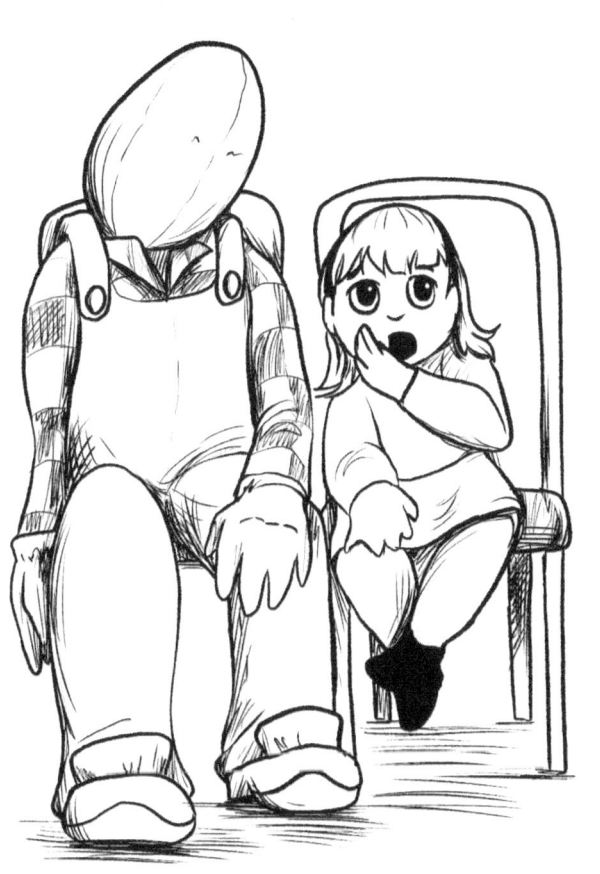

32

We got up early the next morning because Nan wanted to make as many pies as possible for the supper, so folks would get a taste for them and know they were special. Then she'd take orders for Thanksgiving and Christmas. My sifting arms were almost dead when we were through, and I could hardly drag myself out of the tub. All this confirmed why we needed to get the house out of Old Lady Griggs' clutches. Earning the rent money was killing us, and I couldn't go on like this.

"When you're ready, I'll meet you out back," Nan called. She was busy stacking her pies in my wagon.

I met her by the caragana hedge. She was dressed particularly warm. "Why are you wearing that?" I pointed to the sweater from the photo. The one with her father and Old Lady Griggs.

"I have my reasons." Nan's lips thinned.

I was about to tell her she should go into the house and take it off, like she'd have told me, but thought better of it. There had to be a reason. It could have been part of a poorly planned disguise. Maybe it was the only way Nan could face her fellow proletariats after the hair-pulling incident; cocooned in her dead father's warmth.

Nan took the lead, and I pushed the wagon from behind. The two of us started our trek to the community hall. It was as slow as molasses in January, and I thought my back would be permanently hunched by the time we got there. I'd be the only crone in grade two.

"When we get these pies unloaded, you can go play," Nan said.

I said nothing. Nan was trying to get rid of me, but I no longer had friends to play with.

"Did you hear me, Celia?"

"I did."

Nan was satisfied, and I was determined to find out why.

In the hall's kitchen there was all kinds of hubbub. Some ladies going this way, others going that. All wore aprons, but none sweaters. Archibald's mom was the first to approach Nan.

"I wish it had been me," she said, kissing Nan on the cheek. "I've wanted to yank out Fanny Figgler's hair ever since the old bat moved in."

Nan's shoulders relaxed, and three more women came and said almost the same thing. Farmer Hempel's wife called Nan her hero. Griggs seemed oblivious to Nan's heroics though. The only thing that concerned her was Nan's sweater. "It's hot as hell in here," Griggs said when she caught sight of us.

Nan nodded and set a pie on the counter, but she didn't take off the oversized sweater.

"You'll be sweating like a pig in no time," Griggs continued, throwing a freshly cut pickle to Mr. Griggs. He was in his usual spot, propped up on a chair in the corner. The pickle bounced off his shirt.

I took the chair next to him. "I'll be your eyes," I whispered, scanning the room.

Mr. Griggs was unresponsive.

"Your wife's talking about hell again." I swung my legs. "And Farmer Hempel's wife just swatted Mrs. Whitford on the backside with a wooden spoon. Now she's pretending it was an accident." More leg swinging. "Nan is heating up in that sweater. Her bangs are starting to stick to her forehead, but it's like she doesn't even notice." I turned Mr. Griggs' eyeless face towards where Nan and Griggs were working at the counter. Griggs was waving a knife through the air as she talked, and Nan was ducking and weaving.

"Molly," Griggs said, loud enough for everyone in the kitchen to hear. "You're going to melt if you don't take that thing off."

Nan pulled the sweater up around her shoulders and did up another button.

"You're as stubborn as an old mule. How you made it this far in life is beyond me." Griggs was going after the pickles like her knife was a guillotine and the green spears were Marie Antoinette. "Don't blame me if you overheat and pass out."

Griggs' words were falling on deaf ears, even though Nan was red in the cheeks and perspiration was ruining her face powder.

That's when Mrs. Whitford sauntered by with Fanny Figgler at her heel. The two were in sync; Mrs. Whitford in her green pencil skirt and Fanny in her orange muumuu—a walking, talking two-headed pumpkin. They both stopped short. "Molly, Fanny's come for an apology."

Nan's eyes didn't even waver. It was like she was in a trance.

"Did you hear me?" Mrs. Whitford's voice rose an octave.

Still Nan didn't stir.

"You're as dense as your granddaughter."

That got Nan's attention. She turned on the pair with

murder in her eyes and one of her homemade pies in each hand. In unison, the pair stepped back. Nan raised the pies.

"This is neither the time nor the place, Molly Canterberry!" Mrs. Whitford's lips had disappeared.

"Time and place for what?" Nan asked.

"For whatever you have planned."

"You have no idea what I have planned." Nan looked Fanny up and down. "But since I see there are no hatpins, perhaps Fanny will try to set fire to the church again."

"What are you talking about?"

"Your fellow PIS lady, Fanny Figgler, formerly known as Fanny *Shandell*, has a history in that department. You should ask her about it."

Mrs. Whitford turned on Fanny. "Shandell. That name sounds familiar."

Fanny went white. "I can explain."

"No need," Mrs. Whitford snapped. "I remember my mother talking about that. I was supposed to be the baby Jesus that year."

I thought Mrs. Whitford was going to throw herself at Fanny Figgler and wrestle her right there in amongst the pots and pans. Instead, she stepped into her, showing her teeth. "You're a full-grown woman. Next time, don't come running to me. Get your own apology."

"What about Brian? What about the Luger?" The words floundered on Fanny's lips.

Nan narrowed her gaze. "Are you threatening me?"

Fanny blinked rapidly. "No."

"Sounds like a threat." Nan took a step closer.

Fanny looked dumbfounded. She turned and scurried out of the kitchen after Mrs. Whitford.

"Molly!" Griggs grabbed Nan by the shoulders and gave her a shake. "Are you listening to me? Take that sweater off!" Poor

Griggs had been oblivious to the whole showdown with Fanny; she was still fixated on Nan's sweater. But then she paused and her eyes glazed over. She looked from the buttons on Nan's dad's sweater to her husband's eyeless face. "Oh, Molly." Her tone had grown soft and whispery. "How could I have forgotten?"

With a sigh of relief, Nan unbuttoned the sweater. "It took you long enough, Dorigen."

Griggs blinked away tears. "It was the greed. It overtook my good judgement. Judgement I've prided myself on my whole life."

Nan nodded and looked from Griggs to her nylon-stuffed husband. "We all know about your judgement."

"I'll put things to right, Molly. I promise. I'll speak to the mayor tomorrow and sign the deed over to you. I'll force-feed him my shepherd's pie casserole if I have to." Griggs fingered one of the buttons on the sweater. "But don't expect me to hug you. With all that sweating, you smell like a rabbit in heat."

When it was time to dish up, Nan filled two plates. I followed her to the back door. Through the screen we could see Mr. Douglas waiting under the old elm at the back of the lot.

"A crack in the teacup," I said.

"No truer words were ever spoken." With her hip, Nan pushed open the door and went to join him.

33

"Hold him still." Griggs glared at Nan. In one hand she held a button, in the other a needle and thread.

"I am." Nan was sitting in the middle of Griggs' kitchen floor, Mr. Griggs' head in her lap.

"Well, you could have fooled me."

I knew Nan was doing her best to bite her tongue. She couldn't tell Griggs that her husband was a stuffed effigy; Griggs found the word 'effigy' offensive. I saw her hit Farmer Hempel over the head with her purse when he called Mr. Griggs that one Sunday. It was the best part of the service.

"When I said I'd help you, I didn't think it was going to be such an ordeal."

"Not an ordeal?" Griggs fumed. "Open-eyed surgery with no anesthesia? Are you insane? Of course, it's an ordeal."

Nan took a deep breath. "Do you want me to do it?"

"No, I just need a little something to steady my nerves."

Griggs leaned forward and put her forehead against Nan's. That's when I knew, whether they liked it or not, they'd always hide each other's eggs.

With a spring in my step, I slipped upstairs, and with my ballpoint pen, I put a line through the first item on my headboard list: *Get Nan's house back.*

34

The Happy Valley Journal was spread out on the table when I strolled into the kitchen.

"I can't believe it made the paper." Griggs' gnarled finger jabbed the page.

Nan leaned over. "I plead the fifth."

Griggs laid a hand on Nan's arm. "Molly Canterberry, you never cease to amaze me."

I pulled up a chair to see what all the fuss was about. It was Oswald Elliot's cartoon strip. In one box Griggs was shaking one side of my deed head and Mayor Forde the other. Nan was beaming, not caring that I was being jostled around. In the next box, Nan and the mayor were about to come to blows. Steam was coming out of Nan's ears and the mayor's eyes were bulging out of his head. I was tucked into Nan's back pocket, as snug as a bug in a rug.

As things will right, the streets of Happy Valley can once more rest at ease. "I knew from the start," said Mayor Forde, placing a hand the size of a small ham on Molly Canterberry's shoulder, "That I could not rest until Molly Canterberry was exonerated. Her name has been dragged through the mud long enough." He scratches his enormous breadbasket, stretching his polyester shirt taut, leaving convenient loops between the strained buttons in which the mayor can dip his pinky to extract unwanted belly button lint.

Molly Canterberry stiffens. "Exonerated from what?"

"From whatever you were onerated for." The mayor looks confused. "Weren't you briefed?"

"Briefed?" Molly looks at the mayor incredulously. "When Agnes, your secretary, told me to smile and nod? And make sure I got out of the way before you slapped me on the behind?"

The mayor nods. "Yes, that's office protocol."

Molly Canterberry inhales deeply before stepping into the full glare of his ineptitude. "If you try to lay a hand on me, I'll show you office protocol, you oversized mama's boy!"

Mayor Forde, taken aback by her unladylike attitude, raises his hands in the air. "Hold on there, little lady. I was just doing my job."

"Don't little lady me!" All the years of pent-up spinsterhood frustrations bubble to the surface. "Building a prison next to a school, was that part of your job?"

The mayor beams with pride. "Innovative thinking."

"So the inmates can slip notes to the children and send you secret communications?"

"What notes?"

"Don't pretend you don't know. Celia brought one to your office. Gave it to Agnes."

"Agnes," Mayor Forde booms. "Get in here."

Agnes Obermeyer shuffles into the office, a crinkled cigarette hanging from her lipsticked lip. "Your Lordship?"

"What's this I hear about a note?"

"I put it in the God-appointed-mayor drawer."

Beads of sweat appear on his furrowed brow.

"No one ever told me there was a God-appointed–mayor drawer."

Agnes casually leans in the doorway. "Well, if you were truly God-appointed, you'd know about it, wouldn't you?"

"How many notes are there?"

"How high can you count?"

As the mayor's fury turns on Agnes, Molly Canterberry slips out of his office and into a crisp autumn day, her granddaughter fast asleep in her hip pocket, her deed head bobbing contentedly with each step. The last thing they hear is the mayor bellowing, "Well which one is it?"

"I think it's the one that smells like pee."

Nan looked up from the strip. "It could have been worse. You never know with Oswald Elliot."

"I suppose," Griggs said. "But as I remember it, I did a lot more than shake the mayor's hand. I trod on his toe and spilt my coffee on the carpet. Those things were pivotal in building tension, setting the scene."

Nan's eyes went wide. "Yes, pivotal."

"What do you think Oswald will write about next?" I asked.

Griggs tilted her head from side to side. "Likely the Halloween Spooktacular. That's always good for a laugh."

I couldn't help but smile inside. Miss Dobbs had said our class was going to perform at the Spooktacular and there was a cash prize. I'd put on a performance all right. The PIS Ladies would never see it coming. And if I played my cards right, I'd win back Archibald, crush Eugenia, and get another sidewalk star, all in one fell swoop. Backing away from the kitchen table, where Nan and Griggs were still going over the strip, I slipped up to my room. I had some planning to do.

A PEEK AT CELIA'S NEXT ADVENTURE
MIDNIGHT HAGS

MIDNIGHT HAGS
CHAPTER ONE

Nan cleared her throat before licking her forefinger. I almost squealed. This was the best time of day. As of late, Nan had doubled our reading time. And all because my best friend, Archibald Quigley, had thrown me over for Eugenia Whitford, the niece of my number one nemesis, Mrs. Whitford. Enid Whitford was not only the pharmacist's wife and my nan's employer; she was also a founding member of The Ladies of the Perpetual Indigence Society. Those PIS ladies—an association with the most regrettable acronym—had it in for my nan, and under the watchful eye of Mrs. Whitford mocked her at every opportunity. They'd dismiss Nan entirely, if she ever acknowledged them long enough to give them a chance. She didn't. And now Eugenia, the pissy niece of that despicable woman, had barged uninvited into my life and stolen my best friend.

All through first grade Archibald and me—yes, I know it's Archibald and *I*, but that's just too formal considering the warmth of our friendship—merrily bumped along, holding hands and swinging arms. We were as snug as two bugs in a rug. We did all the things normal friends do: dredged mud puddles for waterlogged earthworms, Frankenstein-walked at dawn, and played Jane Eyre when we were out on a stroll. (I was Jane, *obviously*, and Archibald the sickly Helen. Helen was a better match for Archibald's pallid complexion.) But then, at the start of Grade Two, in stepped Eugenia Whitford, and I was unceremoniously tossed on the refuse pile of humanity, right beside Timmy Crybaby-Head.

Cleaved from my bosom buddy at the dawn of second grade, I witnessed the remnants of my friendship with Archibald dashed upon the dusty chalkboard of an inadequate education. It wasn't just Archibald I'd been separated from; it was her entire family. Not to mention the magnificent doors to her family's library, with their carved wooden panels and brass door knockers in the shape of hands holding apples. Just thinking about it made my breath catch. But worst of all, I wouldn't be able to marvel at her magnificent mantel clock, the greatest treasure of all Happy Valley. The one Archibald's last dad ordered for her mom, hoping it would stretch out their days together. But alas, it was for naught. His days were as pinched as those of all the other husbands who came before him. Now he's dead and buried, with the rest of that unlucky crew, in the Happy Valley Graveyard, three graves down from Archibald's original dad.

My lip quivered at the thought of them. All those cold bodies lying side by side, each one dying in his own peculiar way, leaving poor Lacey—whatever her last name was at the time—to give birth to another fatherless child. It was why Archibald carried her father's given name, a living tribute to a man who would never see her face.

To comfort myself, I closed my eyes and envisioned that Prague Clock—the clock that was supposed to change everything. Its face was flanked by the characters of Miser, holding a bag of gold; Vanity, holding a mirror, and Worldly Pleasure, playing a lute. Last but not least was the skeleton—Death—that held an hourglass in one hand and a bell in the other. The bell rang at the top of the hour. The sound pealed through the air, telling Miser, Vanity and Worldly Pleasure that their time was up. In unison, the three amigos would shake their heads no, as if this would stave off the inevitable. I still shake my head whenever I think a clock might be chiming somewhere, just in case those three delinquents know something I don't.

The thought of Eugenia touching the brass door knocker, and breathing the air of unread books, while she listened to Archibald recite her little clock spiel—the one she'd memorized from the World Book Encyclopedia—cut me to the quick.

In my mind, unevolved Eugenia would yawn and roll her eyes. *That's nothing*, she'd say, interrupting Archibald. *We have a better clock at home. My dad ordered it from the Simpson-Sears catalogue. It has the cutest little bird that comes out, flaps its tiny wings, and tweets. Not some stupid old men wrapped up in bedsheets. They look like hippies.*

I squeezed the girls from my thoughts and turned back to Nan. She was going on and on about something I wasn't paying attention to. I smiled and nodded, letting her know I believed in her, and that what she was spouting probably had some merit. When she was satisfied she'd made her point, she opened the cover of our next adventure.

Nan didn't read me regular kid books, like *Charlie and the Chocolate Factory* or *The Giving Tree*. In fact, when the school librarian sent home *The Giving Tree*, with a note saying she hoped I'd find it inspiring, Nan was livid. She flipped through the book, grunting on almost every page. "I don't want you reading this," she said.

"Why not?"

She slapped the book shut. "Have I taught you nothing? All the reading and prodding. Your endless interruptions and questions?"

I shrugged.

Nan groaned through her indignation. "Did you really look at what this book's about? At first glance it can seem quite sweet. Unconditional love at its finest. But that's not what's happening. The tree gives and gives of itself until there is nothing left but a stump. Yet the boy doesn't notice, let alone acknowledge what he's taken. It hurts my heart, Celia. You know how many women have lived lives like that? Thinking it's the right thing to do? Letting a man whittle them down to nothing?"

I shrugged.

"Too many. And only the men that have whittled them down to nothing are remembered." The vein in her neck pulsed. "I have never sanctioned book burning, but if ever there was a book that needed to be thrown on a pyre, it's this one."

When I told the school librarian what Nan had said, her lips thinned. "When your grandmother becomes the literary maven of Happy Valley, I'll take her opinion seriously. But until then she should keep her trap shut." She tossed *The Giving Tree* onto the return cart and lowered her voice. "But don't tell her I said so."

That's why Nan insisted on the classics. She said books were like fellow travellers, and if I were going to keep company with someone else's imaginings, she didn't want it to be sentimental claptrap.

"I think you'll discover," Nan said, draping an arm across my shoulders, "that there are some book people you'll love more than regular people."

I blinked hard. "Are there book people you love more than me?"

Nan gave a dry snort. "Celia, you're the living embodiment of a book person. As if you strolled right off the page and onto my lap."

I leaned into her, blushing at the compliment. Nan knew me too well. We were two book people snuggled under a blanket, whiling away our time. I glanced up to her with adoration. "Do you ever sneak into my room when I'm not there and talk to Captain Ahab?" He was one of my favourite book people. Ever since Nan read Moby Dick to me, Captain Ahab and Queequeg have lived on my sailboat bed.

"No," she said, a smile playing at the edges of her mouth.

Somehow I didn't believe her; Captain Ahab had a way with older women. I snuggled closer and inhaled Nan's essence. Luckily for me she smelled better than Anna Karenina, who was languishing in the root cellar.

Nan was the only person in Happy Valley who understood how I could drift between storybook people and breathing ones, and knew that any time, day or night, they could fill my empty spaces and sit silently with me in my loneliness. Even Archibald, when we were still friends, couldn't do that. If I ever snuck into her house in the middle of the night to shake her awake so she could help me sit in my gloom, she'd likely scream bloody murder. Then punch me in the head.

Nan interrupted my musings. "A penny for your thoughts."

I shrugged. There weren't enough pennies in the world to cover my misery. Even with Nan's extra readings, I didn't know how I was going to manage the rest of second grade. No best friend. No one to play with on my sailboat bed with Captain Ahab. And to top it all off, my teacher, Miss Dobbs, hated me. She never said it out loud, except when she was giving a spelling test. "*Hate. I hate Celia Canterberry. H-a-t-e.*" And that wasn't the worst of it. Guess who her new pet was? Yep. The Usurper. Eugenia Whitford.

Nan paused and waggled an eyebrow before scanning a page in *The Scarlet Pimpernel*. "Where did we leave Lady Blakeney?"

I let out a deep breath. "I don't want to hurt your feelings, Nan, but Lady Blakeney is disappointing." I didn't tell her that Captain Ahab agreed. Last night on my sailboat bed, when the moon peeked between the bedsheet sails I'd tied to the curtain rod, Captain Ahab chewed the inside of his cheek. "Some of the books your nan reads you—you know, with fainting women that are all fluff and curls—well, the lot of them could curdle milk." He slipped a knife out of his pocket and began sharpening a willow stick. "Where are the women who took up the sword? Stormed castles? Slipped in and out of the shadows, not leaving a track in their wake?"

I shrugged. "Nan doesn't want to give me any ideas."

Captain Ahab went quiet for a long time. "Queequeg"—that's what he called me— "Queequeg, let me tell you something. If you need ideas, I'm your man."

Nan grunted. "I thought you were enjoying *The Scarlet Pimpernel*?"

"The Pimpernel, yes. But his wife is supposed to be the most witty and clever woman in the world, and I haven't laughed once. And if she's so clever, why does she do such stupid things?"

Nan sucked her teeth. "You may have a point. But you must remember things were different back then. Women didn't have the right to vote, make their own decisions or have their own money. Men ruled the roost. Our world has changed, and so have our women."

"Just like *The Giving Tree*." I was starting to hate that book.

"For the most part." There was hesitation in Nan's voice.

"But not all women fit that mold. There was Emmeline Pankhurst, Marie Curie, and Jane Austen. Remember *Pride and Prejudice*?"

I nodded.

"That was Austen at her finest. We'll read more from her. And we shouldn't forget Nahdeste, Geronimo's wise sister. And of course Boudicca."

"Boudicca." The name caught on my earlobe and swung itself into my brain. "Who was she?"

"Queen of the Celts, a fierce warrior. She gave Rome a run for its money."

I said her name again. "I bet Captain Ahab would like her."

"I'm afraid Boudicca might make short work of Captain Ahab." Nan cleared her throat. "Are you ready to hear more of Sir Percy Blakeney and Marguerite St. Just?"

I nodded. Despite my disappointment in Lady Blakeney, my curiosity got the best of me.

"*Marguerite listened—half-dazed as she was—to the fast-retreating, firm footsteps of the four men.*

"*All nature was so still that she, lying with her ear close to the ground, could distinctly trace the sound of their tread, as they ultimately turned into the road, and presently the faint echo of the old cart-wheels, the halting gait of the lean nag, told her that her enemy was a quarter of a league away. How long she lay there she knew not. She had lost count of time; dreamily she looked up at the moonlit sky, and listened to the monotonous roll of the waves.*"

As Nan read, my mind wandered. Boudicca was shuffling through my thoughts, finding a place where Captain Ahab hadn't taken up residence. They would make a formidable pair. This should have made me jump for joy, but it didn't. What if Boudicca looked around, was unimpressed, and decided not to take up residence? What if she caught a whiff of Eugenia and preferred her, just like Archibald did? What if she convinced Captain Ahab to weigh anchor and heave ho off to the Whitfords'? Poor Queequeg would be devastated. But not as much as me.

Enjoyed the peek? **Buy Midnight Hags today!**
  https://cphoff.com/books/

ABOUT THE ILLUSTRATOR

Michelle has always had a love for horses and animals that has influenced her artwork since she could first hold a pencil. She first discovered digital art in 2007 and has never looked back since.

She grew up in Brooks, Alberta, and has attended schools in Vancouver, California and Montreal where she has learned how to cultivate her creativity and improve both herself and her craft.

In addition to animals and creatures, she is also inspired by movies, video games and fantasy fiction. She is excited to someday start an independent project where she can illustrate and write full-time.

To see more of her artwork visit www.michellefroese.com

HELLO MY WONDERFUL READER,

Thanks for reading *A Crack in the Teacup*. If you enjoyed your time with Celia, a review would be much appreciated as it helps other readers discover the story.

If you have a minute sign up for my intrepid newsletter. Each month, I herald one of my beloved words or turns of phrase, and in turn, you are invited to herald right back. And if your phrase or word is not one I've considered, or one that someone else has suggested, it may end up in my next work of fiction (with an acknowledgement of its sender tucked firmly within the yarn's pages).

I look forward to hearing from you. Thanks again.

All my best,

C.P. Hoff

Join my email list:

www.cphoff.com

CONTENTS

The Happy Valley Chronicles	iii
Dear Reader	ix
Books By CP Hoff	xi
Chapter 1	1
Chapter 2	14
Chapter 3	20
Chapter 4	30
Chapter 5	40
Chapter 6	50
Chapter 7	58
Chapter 8	62
Chapter 9	70
Chapter 10	78
Chapter 11	84
Chapter 12	90
Chapter 13	100
Chapter 14	110
Chapter 15	114
Chapter 16	118
Chapter 17	124
Chapter 18	132
Chapter 19	136
Chapter 20	148
Chapter 21	154
Chapter 22	160
Chapter 23	166
Chapter 24	172
Chapter 25	178
Chapter 26	184
Chapter 27	194
Chapter 28	200

Chapter 29	206
Chapter 30	214
Chapter 31	218
Chapter 32	222
Chapter 33	228
Chapter 34	232
A peek at Celia's next adventure	235
Midnight Hags	239
ABOUT THE ILLUSTRATOR	247
Hello my wonderful Reader,	249

www.ingramcontent.com/pod-product-compliance
Lightning Source LLC
LaVergne TN
LVHW041625060526
838200LV00040B/1433